Women in Game Development

BREAKING THE GLASS LEVEL-CAP

Women in Game Development

BREAKING THE GLASS LEVEL-CAP

EDITED BY
JENNIFER BRANDES HEPLER

CRC Press
Taylor & Francis Group
Boca Raton London New York

CRC Press is an imprint of the
Taylor & Francis Group, an **informa** business

AN A K PETERS BOOK

CRC Press
Taylor & Francis Group
6000 Broken Sound Parkway NW, Suite 300
Boca Raton, FL 33487-2742

© 2017 by Taylor & Francis Group, LLC
CRC Press is an imprint of Taylor & Francis Group, an Informa business

No claim to original U.S. Government works

Printed on acid-free paper
Version Date: 20160509

International Standard Book Number-13: 978-1-138-94792-4 (Paperback)

This book contains information obtained from authentic and highly regarded sources. Reasonable efforts have been made to publish reliable data and information, but the author and publisher cannot assume responsibility for the validity of all materials or the consequences of their use. The authors and publishers have attempted to trace the copyright holders of all material reproduced in this publication and apologize to copyright holders if permission to publish in this form has not been obtained. If any copyright material has not been acknowledged please write and let us know so we may rectify in any future reprint.

Library of Congress Cataloging-in-Publication Data

Names: Hepler, Jennifer Brandes, author.
Title: Women in game development : breaking the glass level-cap / Jennifer Brandes Hepler.
Description: Boca Raton, FL : CRC Press, 2017. | Includes index.
Identifiers: LCCN 2016013699 | ISBN 9781138947924 (alk. paper)
Subjects: LCSH: Video games industry. | Computer software developers. | Women in computer science. | Sex discrimination in employment.
Classification: LCC HD9993.E452 H47 2017 | DDC 331.4/817948--dc23
LC record available at https://lccn.loc.gov/2016013699

Visit the Taylor & Francis Web site at
http://www.taylorandfrancis.com

and the CRC Press Web site at
http://www.crcpress.com

Printed and bound in the United States of America by Sheridan

This book is dedicated to the tens of thousands of women who have been toiling invisibly in the game industry since it began. We couldn't fit you all in here, but we know that every one of your stories is unique and valuable and part of what makes games into the art form that we all love. Thank you all for doing what you do.

Contents

Acknowledgments

This project has been a delight to work on, from beginning to end. There's nothing like being able to say, "Hey, do you want to be in my book?", to allow you to cold-call some of the people you respect the most in your field. And after collaborating with them and sharing in their wonderful stories, I feel like they all have become friends.

So, first, a huge thanks to all of my amazing contributors and also to the many other inspiring women who offered stories that we didn't have the space to include. Special thanks to Judy Tyrer, Brianna Wu, Jane Ng, Kimberly Unger, Elizabeth LaPensée, Elizabeth Sampat, Megan Gaiser, Sheri Rubin, Mattie Brice, and my fantastic company, Kognito Interactive, for also providing your additional artwork and photos to give the book some visual flair.

A thousand thanks to our cover artist, Kimberly Unger, who after I spent months tearing my hair out about how to visually represent women in games without showing a pink game controller, knocked it out of the park with her adorable pixel-lady.

And special thanks to Sheri Rubin who proved that QA truly runs in her blood by reviewing the entire manuscript with a fine-toothed comb. The book is far better for having had your eye on it!

I am also grateful to Sean Connelly and everyone at CRC Press for supporting this project from the very first letter I sent about it. You've been great to work with. Let's do this again someday!

And on a personal note, I could never have juggled my job, freelance work, family life, and this book without the constant support of my parents, Sue and Larry Brandes, my husband, Chris Hepler, and my wonderful kids, Beverly and Shane.

One thing I've been thinking about this past week is the unique challenges women face in the virtual world…. We know that women gamers face harassment and stalking and threats of violence from other players. When they speak out about their experiences, they're attacked on Twitter and other social media outlets, even threatened in their homes.

What's brought these issues to light is that there are a lot of women out there, especially young women, who are speaking out bravely about their experiences, even when they know they'll be attacked for it—from feminist bloggers who refuse to be silenced, to women sports reporters who are opening up about the extreme safety precautions they need to take when traveling for work. Every day, women of all ages and all backgrounds and walks of life are speaking out. And by telling their stories, by you telling your stories, women are lifting others out of the shadows and raising our collective consciousness about a problem that affects all of us.

President Barack Obama
White House Reception for Women's History Month
March 16, 2016

Contributors

Leigh Alexander
Journalist

Mattie Brice
Independent

Megan Gaiser
Contagious Creativity

Rebecca Ann Heineman
Olde Sküül

Jennifer Brandes Hepler
Kognito Interactive

Erin Hoffman-John
GlassLab Games

Laura Hudson
Wired and Offworld.com

Elizabeth LaPensée
Independent

Laralyn McWilliams
The Workshop Entertainment

Jane Ng
Campo Santo

Katie Postma
Disruptor Beam

Donna Prior
En Masse Entertainment

Sheri Graner Ray
Zombie Cat Studios

Brenda Romero
Romero Games

Sheri Rubin
Design Direct Deliver

Elizabeth Sampat
Electronic Arts

Anita Sarkeesian
Feminist Frequency

Kari Toyama
Valve Software

Judy Tyrer
3 Turn Productions

Kimberly Unger
Bushi-go, Inc.

Karisma Williams
Independent

Brianna Wu
Giant Spacekat

1

Introduction

"Full disclosure" is a term that gets thrown around a lot recently regarding game journalism. So, in the interests of full disclosure, let me say that I knew none of the amazing women in this book until quite recently. In fact, until they began to face a sustained campaign of harassment to try to drive them out of gaming, it's safe to say that most women in the industry toiled alone, knowing they loved games and wanted to devote their lives to making them, but not how many other women were harboring the exact same dreams.

But as women have been targeted, harassed, threatened with death and rape on a regular basis, faced with an anonymous mob of so-called "fans" who want to drive them out of their jobs, the natural thing has been to reach out to each other. Those who were the earliest victims reached out to comfort those suddenly in the spotlight. And communities of support sprang up everywhere.

Suddenly, instead of working alone, women in gaming were part of a vast network of supporters reaching out to them, face-to-face or online, across companies and countries, publicly on Twitter, or behind closed doors. #1reasonwhy became a Twitter phenomenon that let women voice the horrifying things said or done to them as a result of wanting to be in the game industry. But that gave way to #1reasontobe, an outpouring of women's love for games, which spawned panels at places such as Geek Girl Con and GDC[1] to give women a chance to voice what they love best about game development and why they stick with it.

And people whose lives were turned upside down by harassment emerged to find themselves celebrities, a new thing in the world—celebrity feminist game developers!—and in turn reached out to others, to encourage them to keep trying for their dreams. So, though the dreaded "feminist illuminati" never really existed, that very fear has now created a community of female game developers determined to see each other succeed. A group of women who reach out to each other when someone is targeted, who support each other through Patreon and other services during the endemic post-project layoffs. A group of women who come from every discipline in gaming, from industry veterans who have weathered gaming's ups and downs since the 1980s, to rising stars who have burst onto the scene in the last few years.

This book just scratches the surface of the thousands of intelligent, talented, hard-working, and opinionated women who can be found in the ranks of nearly every game company. They have come together to tell you their stories—why they wanted to be in games, how they broke in, the obstacles they've faced, and what keeps them coming in to work every morning, even on the bad days.

If you are a woman, working in or hoping to break into game development, this is the chance you've always wanted to corner some of your inspirations at a conference and hear what they have to say in an unguarded moment. If you're a man in the industry, these are the stories your female colleagues want you to hear, so that you understand that the struggles they face working in games are different than what you see, and they need your support. And if the first time you heard about women in gaming was on *The Colbert Report* or *Law & Order: Special Victims Unit*, these are stories you should hear to understand how one of the twenty-first century's fastest-growing forms of entertainment can sometimes be so hostile to the women who create it that they have had to flee their homes in fear of their lives.

In these pages, 22 women in game development tell you their experiences in their own words. In addition, this book provides further information about the latest research on related topics, such as how unconscious gender bias affects people during hiring and corporate reviews, what Imposter Syndrome is and how it can affect talented women, and what really happened during the ongoing harassment campaign known as "Gamergate." And if you're one of those crazy enough or passionate enough to pursue a career in games despite the costs, you'll find tips for breaking into many fields of development, from design and writing, to programming, art, community management, production, and quality assurance. And you can go in armed with the knowledge that even if it gets bad, there are women who have fought those same battles for years and they will welcome you with open arms.

So, pull up a chair, turn the page, and imagine you're at GDC, at the best mixer ever, where no one interrupts and the music isn't too loud.

And you're getting the chance to meet some of the best and brightest ladies in the industry, one-on-one. What can they tell you?

Is This a Feminist Book?

Is this a feminist book? How could it not be? Feminism is the belief that women are equal to men, that their ideas and experiences are worth hearing about, that they deserve and will succeed at any of the same opportunities given to men. Writing this book is an act of feminism just like voting, or sending your daughter to college, or celebrating your wife's promotion. This is the feminism that the great majority of both men and women in the developed world believe in, often without thinking about it.

However, there is also the more academic meaning of the word *feminism*. This is the feminism of Gender Studies classes, and while it is important, it can tend to operate in a rarified sphere of specialized language that can be confusing or off-putting if you're not used to it.

The women in this book are, for the most part, not academics (though a few are). They have written their stories in the language of programmers, business people, game designers, writers. They have written their opinions, their life experiences, their lessons learned. And in some cases, they have written things that disagree with each other.

This is one of the biggest misunderstandings about feminism. There are those who see, for example, two female game developers, one criticizing *Grand Theft Auto* and one loving it, and call that proof that feminism is meaningless. That couldn't be further from the truth. The truth of feminism is that women are people, with tastes and opinions as wildly divergent as men's.

So is this book feminist? Of course it is. No book designed to highlight the achievements of women could be anything else. But it is, first and foremost, a "boots on the ground" view of game development, written by women actually working in the field.

Endnote

1. The Game Developers Conference, the largest professional gathering of game developers.

2

Brenda Romero

Games: *Train, Síochán Leat, Wizardry: Proving Grounds of the Mad Overlord, Wizardry II: The Knight of Diamonds, Wizardry III: Legacy of Llylgamyn, Wizardry IV: The Return of Werdna, Wizardry V: Heart of the Maelstrom, Wizardry VI: Bane of the Cosmic Forge, Wizardry VII: Crusaders of the Dark Savant, Wizardry 8, Wizardry Gold, Nemesis: The Wizardry Adventure, Jagged Alliance, Jagged Alliance: Deadly Games, Jagged Alliance 2, Jagged Alliance 2: Unfinished Business, Realms of Arkania Vol. 1: Blade of Destiny, Tom Clancy's Ghost Recon: Commander, Realms of Arkania Vol. 2: Star Trail, Druid: Daemons of the Mind, Freakin' Funky Fuzzballs, Dungeons & Dragons: Heroes, Playboy: The Mansion, Playboy: The Mansion Party Pak, Def Jam: Icon, The Walking Dead, PreConception, Pettington Park, Retro City Rampage, Ravenwood Fair, Ravenstone Mine, Critter Island, Garden Life, SuperPoke Pets,*

SPP Ranch, Top Fish, Rescue Raiders, Crypt of Medea (Some credited as Brenda Brathwaite or Brenda Garno)

Books: *Sex in Video Games, Challenges for Game Designers, Breaking into the Game Industry*

Before I say anything else, let me say this: I am profoundly grateful for a life spent in the game industry. I cannot imagine any other way of life. It is the culture in which I was raised and, barring some last-minute career change, it is the culture in which I will die. It is here that I find the soul of my creativity, my closest friends, my inspirations, and my loves. It really is who I am, and for all the criticisms one may throw at it, the game industry is my home.

Second-Hand Games

I started making games when I was five, I think. My mother would bring me to garage sales, and since we didn't have much money, I would pick out second-hand games. The cheapest ones were those that were missing a few parts. I didn't much mind, actually. I'd collect the parts and recycle them into my own games. At such a young age, the "games" didn't have rules, per se, but they did have narrative structures or ways of behaving. At some point, I discovered LEGOs, and realized I could create entire worlds with them. I'd spend hours creating complex areas, what I would now call "levels," and invite my family to go through them while I played the role of narrator guiding them down hallways, past spooky corners, and into the un-adventured and unknown.

This desire to create worlds, a phrase that the late, great Origin Systems used as their corporate tagline, eventually extended to writing. My friends and I would rush home from school and gather around one or another's kitchen table and spend hours creating and exchanging stories. With nothing else to fill the space, we filled it with our own creativity. I remember writing plays which we staged with neighborhood kids for their parents in someone's basement. From offstage, I watched the audience react to what I'd created. It is that feeling which I chase in games to this day.

My magical moment as a gamer came when my mother got me the original white box version of *Dungeons & Dragons*. Three books, two dice, and a pencil, and I was gone. It was the perfect mix of my interests—storytelling and games. In those pages, I found a structure in which I could absolutely lose myself. I'd spend hours creating characters and worlds, complete stories for people to play. Better yet, these were not small, discrete events. The worlds and characters that I created extended far beyond a single session.

In playing *Dungeons & Dragons*, I felt as if something had been created just for me. By the time I was fourteen, I was in the thick of it and had begun to explore systems other than D&D. By then, Iron Crown's *Rolemaster* system was my system of choice, and in a move that foretold my career more than any other, I decided to rewrite the rules of encumbrance (how much your character can carry and how it affects them). Unfortunately, that little edit required edits to other parts of the system, and before I knew it, I rewrote the whole thing. My friends named it "Brenda Law," and we enjoyed many hours in a system that I am sure was full of holes and flaws overlooked by our forgiving imaginations.

Discovering Video Games

By now, arcades had come to Ogdensburg, New York, and every Saturday, I would faithfully deposit my allowance into the machines, quarter-by-quarter, until it was gone. *Pac-Man*, *Tron*, and *Ms. Pac-Man* were my favorites. I was mesmerized by the darkness of the arcades, the bar-like atmosphere. That parents didn't want their kids in there only made us all want to be there even more.

Yet, there was something beyond playing games that drove me, a curiosity about how things worked, coupled with a need to create my own worlds. Though I had no idea how something as complicated as a video arcade game was made, I imagined (incorrectly, it turns out) that inside those cabinets were the same tangle of wires that I'd seen inside pinball machines. I had no concept that I could create something like that—an actual game—on the VIC-20 my mother had just purchased for me at home.

It's interesting for me to look back on this. We didn't have much, my mom and me. My dad had passed away when I was just four, leaving my mom alone with three kids. At this time, one of us was in college and another heading there soon. How my mom had enough money for this, I don't know, but she certainly got her money's worth. I became as obsessed with programming as I was with playing games. I dutifully typed in programs from magazines I got at the library and modified the code to make the program do something different. I signed up for the new programming class at my high school, learned BASIC, and took my first tentative steps into Pascal. If I had to do anything more than two times, I'd code it instead. Code did the same thing for me that board game parts did, that writing did, that D&D did—it gave me a framework in which to create worlds.

By this point, I had become very much the person I still am today: a girl, now woman, obsessed with games, technology, metal music, and classic cars. Everything and nothing has changed.

Sir-Tech Software

In the fall of 1981, while smoking in the bathroom at my local high school, another student came in looking for a cigarette. Now, before I go further, I must tell you that (a) you shouldn't smoke, (b) it was dumb that I smoked at all, (c) we smoked in the bathroom against the school's policy, and (d) we were prohibited from leaving the building during school hours without prior permission (and no, they wouldn't grant permission to go outside and smoke, so you can perhaps understand the idiotic nicotine addict's dilemma here).

That girl was Linda Sirotek, then 15 herself, and co-owner of Sir-tech Software, one of the game industry's very first companies and publisher of the amazing *Wizardry* series of role-playing games (RPGs). It was obvious to me that Linda was looking for a non-menthol cigarette, and so I offered her one. To be polite, she struck up a conversation. "Do you have a job?" she asked. I didn't. "Have you heard of Sir-tech?" she said. Again, I hadn't. "Have you played D&D?"

Oh.

With that, my job interview concluded, and I agreed to meet Linda at her house the following Tuesday to play *Wizardry* for the first time. To say that this was the beginning of a long, long love affair is to minimize the effect of *Wizardry* and Sir-tech on my life. Here at last was everything—all of it— that I loved: storytelling, games, D&D, and technology.

I was hired by Sir-tech on October 6, 1982, at the ripe old age of 15. While there, I was blessed to work with such incredibly talented people, from Robert Woodhead and Andrew Greenberg to David Bradley, Ian Currie, and Linda herself. It was a small company and a small industry then. I was very isolated from the rest of the industry in Ogdensburg, so whatever games and technology I encountered, I encountered through Sir-tech itself. It was a magical, sheltered time, but I was magically sheltered with some of the best game developers in the world working on amazing, award-winning games. What great fortune I had to be in that right place at the right time.

How to Stay

Truth be told, I really do not know how to break in to the game industry, at least from experience. Smoking in the restroom of a high school is more likely to get you in trouble than it is to get you a job. I know the advice I tell others (work hard; learn to code; play games; start making games early, now if possible), but it's a very different industry than when I first started.

What I do know, however, what I know to the core of my being is how to stay. As I write this, I've just passed my 34th year in the game industry. I've seen a great many people come and go. I've watched the industry grow from a handful of women into whole conferences dedicated solely to women in games. I've gone from knowing all the women, to mostly everyone, to occasionally no one in a room, and it's wonderful. It's also important that I clarify something: I don't consider myself a "woman in games." I am a person who makes games. My gender is just one thing about me, one I think about very little. I just am who I am.

I am conscious that around me in this book there are stories of others telling you how they got in and offering advice on how you can get in, too. There are stories of people who struggled and people who shined. There are stories of change, of transition, of moving from one part of the industry to the other. There are far more stories than there ever will be games.

But what I know best is how to stay. Here is what I know.

Have Fun

If you're not having fun, odds are you're not going to make your game fun either. Making games is hard work and shipping them is even harder. Company culture is critical to make it work. Be a fun person to be around. Laugh and enjoy your work. Find things to enjoy. There are always things to get frustrated about, but why share the misery? Choose a positive focus and above all, don't take yourself too seriously.

Surround Yourself

Some people have a choice: the game industry or another field? I am not one of those people. I genuinely believe that I was called to games like people are "called to the priesthood." My love for games and for creating worlds within games goes so deep, I just can't imagine what else I would do. As a result, I am incredibly driven by games and by my fascination with them. My life is games—making, playing, and talking about them. My outside interests, more often than not, inspire my games, make them richer or are driven by them.

I need that level of passion around me. I need to turn to my love and be able to have a conversation about a mechanic many would find trivial. I need to share my greatest joys with someone who gets it. The happiest relationships I have seen are those where the partners are both in games or are both equally driven. John[1] and I could be accused of working too much if you were looking from the outside in. But to me, "work" is only what I have to do when I am forced to be someone other than who I am.

Look for a Way to Grow

I got my foot in the door at Sir-tech when I was 15, worked on what was known as the "Wizardry hotline," and spent the next few years of my life doing community support. If you had questions about Wizardry, I had your answer. A whole portion of my brain is still dedicated to remembering unbelievably trivial questions about those games.

When I went to college, I continued to work for Sir-tech, testing games in development and eventually writing the documentation surrounding the games. I constantly looked for new things to learn and new jobs to do, and as a result, I worked my way up into doing product development full time. For me, looking for ways to grow has been critical to remaining happy. I am naturally curious, and I need to learn and to push myself beyond comfortable borders.

Many times, the industry itself will do this for you with new hardware, new demographics, new play styles, new ways of connecting. Other times, it's necessary to do it yourself, as I did when I decided to try my hand at making board games.

Leave

I started at Sir-tech when I was just 15 years old. By the time I left in 2001, 20 years had passed. I'd gone from *Wizardry 1* to *Wizardry 8*, seen the rise and fall of single-player, hard-core RPGs and witnessed the birth of first-person shooters (FPS), massively multiplayer online (MMO) games, mobile games, local area network (LAN) parties, and so much more. I started as a person on Sir-tech's hint line and rose to become a designer on the game series I loved more than any other. I designed dozens of levels, worked alongside others on systems, wrote reams of game text, and planned *Wizardry 8's* entire storyline, walking in the shoes of my one-time mentor, David W. Bradley.

I'd learned so, so much at Sir-tech, but here's the surprising part—maybe I should have left earlier than I did. Twenty years is a long time. It's a long time to learn the same things from the same people. When you're founders and you've been together that long, that's great. When you're an employee without an equity stake? Maybe it's worth expanding your horizons. I never learned faster than when I finally went out on my own. For me, a person who is comfortable in the nest, so to speak, it took me too long to look for new teachers who could expand my horizons and keep me challenged and growing.

Always Fight for the Credits

I learned this from Shawn Lyng, one of the designers of *Jagged Alliance*. Credits are important now, and they are important to your future work. Make sure you get credited for the work that you do.

Seek Mentors

I wish I had learned this one earlier. Always look for someone better than you are at something and actively learn from them. Recently, I've taken this to a very active level and asked fellow game designers for an hour of their time in exchange for an hour of mine. The goal is that we will teach each other about something the other doesn't know or, perhaps, doesn't know as well. I recently asked Chelsea Howe to talk with me about some challenging aspects of mobile game design. I asked Soren Johnson to talk to me about putting people in situations where they have to make difficult decisions in games. Clearly and obviously, I don't know everything. Admitting that I have more to learn is more a reflection of an aspiration toward greatness than it is a weakness. The more you learn, the less you know.

Not Everything Said about You Will Be True

Not everything said about you will be true and not everyone will like you. This is particularly true if you are in the public eye, a lead, a boss, a company owner, or should you be fortunate to become extremely successful in your career as many of my friends have. Sometimes, making a good game means giving people feedback that's difficult to swallow. Sometimes, it means firing people. Sometimes, you have to make decisions based on information you can't share with everyone on the team. Ultimately, I have to be comfortable with the truth I know. Being open-minded goes hand-in-hand with this, of course. If it turns out the truth I know isn't truth, I accept that.

Talk Up

Game development can sometimes be a long, challenging road, and there will come a time when you may find yourself wildly frustrated by your team. When that is the case, talk up. Go to your lead and vent it. I can't stress this enough. Listening to your problems is part of their gig and what they are trained to do. If it's your lead you're frustrated with, go to them first, then someone over them if needed. Whatever you do, don't talk down. The single greatest destroyer of teams and team morale is people trash-talking leads, leadership, or other people on their own team (or other teams, for that matter). Often, those being trashed have no idea what's even happening or how they could alter their behavior to make things better for everyone.

People Have the Freedom to Be Assholes

This is one of the most important pieces of advice I was given, one which I took to heart and one which I still use regularly. People have bad days. People can be incredible, profound tools. They can say things for the express purpose of trying to eviscerate you. They have that freedom. It's not pleasant, but it also is not mine to own or to take on. I will gain nothing if I try to change them, take them on individually, or otherwise attempt to make them anything but what they are. Like a person who screams at you from the side of the road as you're out for a leisurely drive, the world is full of colorful people, but their "colorfulness" doesn't have to affect me. This is particularly important in the age of anonymity. Trying to change assholes is about as useful as arguing with a drunk. Be the example you want to see. Do the things you want others to do.

Learn to Apologize and Be a Better Person, Constantly

Regrettably, we have the freedom to be assholes, too, and it means that from time to time, we are going to screw up. This becomes more and more important the higher you rise in the industry. I've been a lead or a company owner for 20 years now. The list of things I could have done better is a long one.

I'm constantly learning, constantly becoming better, and willing to own up to it when I realize it or when someone comes to me with an example of how I could have done better.

A dear friend of mine has a great line about this. He told me, "If you get on the bus and think everyone's an asshole, maybe it's actually you who's the problem."

Don't Take Shit

I can only stay and continue to make games somewhere I feel creative and passionate and where the team is having fun. If we're not having it, we're not going to make it. Giving people freedom to be assholes doesn't mean you have to stand for being treated poorly. If you find yourself in a situation that is personally or professionally uncomfortable for you, something needs to change.

At times like this, I find my answer in the oddest of places—the old "Serenity Prayer." I am not a religious person by any means, but there's wisdom here. "Grant me the serenity to accept the things I cannot change, the courage to change the things I can, and the wisdom to know the difference."

This brings me back to my two previous points. I've been in situations in which I could change things *without being an asshole*, either in the job, in myself, or in the game. And I've been in situations in which I could not change things.

I have left jobs in which the commute proved to be too long and too dangerous. I've left jobs where the owners treated the employees poorly. I no longer keep company with people around whom I feel unsafe. I ask myself these questions: Does it need to change? Do I need to change it? Do I need to change it right now? Do I need to change it *this way*? You'd be surprised at how often the answer to one of those is no. When it's yes, though, I am on my way.

Remember the Core

In games, the core is the one thing that the game is about, and every feature must make that core stronger. In life, my core is no different. I am here to make games. I could do a great many things, but professionally, games are what I choose to do. That is how I spend my time, and I am aggressively cautious when it comes to feature creep. The older I get, the more I think about this. I'm 49. I only have so many games left in me and so much time to devote to them. What I do, what I choose to take on, it's all zero sum.

Stay in Love with Games and Keep Your Passion

The one abiding thing that will get you through anything this industry throws at you is your passion for games, for the game industry, and for crafting something great. There are times when you may feel like you want to bow out or do something other than make games for a living.

Take a step back and remember greatness, remember why you did this in the beginning. For me, it's that 11-year-old version of me with D&D. She was holding on to those books and a pile of graph paper with worlds in her hands. She believed I could do this, and she still believes.

Stay.

Endnote

1. Editor's Note: Brenda's husband, John Romero, the legendary designer and co-programmer of *Wolfenstein 3D, Doom*, and *Quake*.

3

Rebecca Ann Heineman

Game Designer: *Dragon Wars, Bard's Tale III: The Thief of Fate, Mindshadow*

Programmer: *Bard's Tale Trilogy, Battle Chess: Game of Kings,* and many more

Co-founder: Interplay Productions, Contraband Entertainment, and Olde Sküül

My story begins in pain. My earliest memories are of my father, punishing me for real and imagined offenses. Being beaten, belittled, and abused in every way possible, my feelings of self-worth and value utterly stripped away. I sought escape, both by running away from home, and by visiting a friend who had a collection of Atari 2600 games. He enjoyed the challenge of competing against me in *Slot Racers*.

Although I won constantly, he kept coming back for more, expecting his skills to finally exceed mine. They never did. However, due to my Imposter Syndrome and the low self-worth left by my upbringing, I never accepted that I was actually good at anything, even when my winning streak was almost 100%. In 1980, Atari sponsored a contest to find the best player of *Space Invaders* for the Atari 2600 and my friend dragged me to Topanga Canyon Plaza (now called Westfield Topanga) and entered me into the contest. I played the game for an hour. When I finally turned in a score of over 80,000 points, I was named the winner.

Even holding the certificate stating that I was the Regional Champion of Atari *Space Invaders* for Los Angeles, I couldn't accept I had value. In November 1980, I was flown to New York City to compete in the Nationals, and there I was, looking at the other contestants, each with a parent, while I stood alone, reminded how completely my family had disowned me.

I won. I had my 15 minutes of fame. I went home, sad and lonely, wondering what to do with my life. I spent countless hours teaching myself how to make devices to download and copy Atari cartridges, because I didn't have the money to buy them. It was a chance mention to Arnie Katz of *Electronic Games Magazine* that I had figured out how to program the Atari 2600 that led me to a conversation with Jack and Eric Dott of the Avalon Hill Game Company. The result of that phone call was a job in Towson, Maryland.

I was so desperate to move out of my mother's home that I lied about my age and accepted the job, packed my things into a steamer trunk, and flew to Baltimore with a plane ticket the Dotts sent me. Then I set to work teaching the programmers at Avalon Hill what I knew about the Atari 2600.

My trusty Apple II and a wire wrap tool were my world as I worked on what eventually became *London Blitz* and *Out of Control* for the Atari 2600. Never once did I feel like I was valued, however. I was in my own little world, separate from everyone as I spent all of my waking hours learning how to make the Atari 2600 do new tricks and teaching myself how to program the Commodore VIC-20 and the Atari 400.

I felt unappreciated, so when Time-Warner asked if I'd consider working in New York on a PlayCable system for the Atari 2600, I accepted and left Avalon Hill for New York City. A winter in New York convinced me that I couldn't cut it on the East Coast and I moved back to Los Angeles.

Interplay

When I got back to Los Angeles, my mother had remarried and her husband convinced me to stay with them. He was the first family I had who treated me like a human being. Every time I dropped something, I expected him to reach for a belt to hit me, but he never did. I started to understand that family didn't have to be pain, but I still didn't really know what it meant.

I needed a job, so I asked the hacker community and someone replied saying that Boone Corporation was hiring. I went there and was hired on the spot. This is where I met Brian Fargo, Jay Patel, and Troy Worrell, and when the owner of Boone Corporation decided to move from game development to selling stuff at swap meets, we all were laid off and went on to form Interplay Productions.

Interplay was touch and go for a few years. There was constant pressure to get games out the door quickly so we would have money to make payroll. I created *Mindshadow* and *The Tracer Sanction*, games that gave me a real feeling of pride. But my lack of self-worth kept me from forming bonds with anyone, and it didn't help that everyone at the company was male.

Which brings us to another subject …

I'm a transgender woman, born with wacky DNA and assigned male at birth. Being a woman in a body that looked male was horrible for me. It was the reason my family hated me, why I had few friends, and couldn't cope in social settings. But it did have one advantage: I had male privilege.

Imposter Syndrome

"Imposter Syndrome" is a term first coined by Pauline Rose Clance and Suzanne Imes, who defined it as "an internal experience of intellectual phoniness, which appears to be particularly prevalent and intense among a select sample of high achieving women."[1] Colloquially, it has come to refer to the belief held by many people, particularly women, that they don't deserve the success they've experienced. This can manifest as a great anxiety that you will be unmasked as a fraud, that your work isn't as good as the people you work with, and that you don't deserve credit for the contributions you've made, since "if you didn't do it, someone else would have."

While Imposter Syndrome is not exclusive to women (in fact, 70% of people at least occasionally experience the feeling of being a fraud),[2] it appears more frequently and in more debilitating ways in high-achieving women than in men in equivalent positions. Many of the amazingly accomplished women in this book admit privately to lifelong struggles with Imposter Syndrome, which have them questioning their abilities even after dozens of successes. And they aren't helped by the tendency in the industry for people to assume that a woman at an industry party is a "+1," not a dev herself. Or by fans constantly demanding that any woman calling herself a gamer prove her "geek cred."

If you find that Imposter Syndrome is holding you back from applying for that first game industry job, asking for that well-deserved promotion, pitching your game idea to investors, or even just speaking up at meetings, the following techniques may help:

- *Set Objective Standards:* If you don't have a specific goal in mind, it's always easy to think, "I should have done more." But if you keep specific written goals (i.e., "Design Dungeon 1 Boss fight by May 1"), then you have objective proof to rebut your own feelings of failure.

- *Don't Compare:* Comparing yourself to other people (especially on social media!) is a sure way to feel terrible. Experts warn not to fall into the trap of comparing your inside (how you feel at your worst moments) to other people's outsides (the handpicked photos and profiles they show the world).
- *Do It Anyway:* Women are shown to consistently be less likely than men to apply for jobs if they feel the least bit unqualified for them. There is an oft-quoted statistic from an internal Hewlett Packard study, that "men apply for jobs when they meet 60% of the qualifications, but women only apply if they meet 100% of them."[3] Reach out of your comfort zone and try to do things with a risk of failure—you'll be surprised how often you'll succeed.

Editor

What is male privilege, you ask? Being a woman who was considered male meant my work was accepted and valued for itself, not belittled because of who made it. I've lost count of the number of times I was in a room where all the men thought they were alone and immediately started objectifying women. A "Frat House" mentality prevailed among them and I had to grit my teeth and keep silent, lest they figure out my secret.

Being accepted as "one of the guys," while not being one inside, allowed me to make suggestions to make our games inclusive. However, I was often overruled with the phrase, "Women don't play these games." When I took over the *Bard's Tale* franchise with *Bard's Tale III: The Thief of Fate*, I went against management's "suggestions" and added female player avatars, gendered pronouns, and silently rewrote many pages of dialogue to remove sexist, misogynistic, and anti-LGBT (lesbian, gay, bisexual, and transgender) remarks. When the game shipped, it was so well-received that it eventually was given a place in an art exhibit at the Smithsonian.

I followed it up with *Dragon Wars*, but soon was moved onto working on game ports and technology because I wasn't a "team player." This led to my parting ways with Interplay in 1995. Once that happened, something I didn't expect happened: people wanted to follow me wherever I ended up.

People cared about me? I had made more friends than I realized at Interplay. While I didn't value myself, others did. I was finally able to look at the work I had done, the games I had made at Interplay, and start to believe what my friends were telling me: I had worth.

A New Family

During my time at Interplay, my loneliness threw me into clinical depression. I really couldn't connect with the men of the company, but I connected with their wives. I became great friends with Stephanie, Brian Fargo's wife at the time, and she saw how sad I was. We would talk for hours and she commented how I wasn't like the other men of the office. I so wanted to tell her that I wasn't "one of the men," but fear of losing her friendship kept me silent.

Stephanie had a plan. She introduced me to her housekeeper and we went on a date. The first date was an unmitigated disaster, worthy of a scene in some romantic comedy. However, it led to a second date, and a third, and before I knew it, I was going to be a parent. Going from "forever alone" to getting the news I would be a parent within the span of four weeks was overwhelming to take. I went with the flow and got married, and prepared myself for parenthood.

My life changed once I held my daughter in my arms. It wasn't about me anymore. It was about her. I had to keep going for her. My maternal instincts kicked in and I changed from spending every waking moment writing game engines to making time for this new human being.

Two years later, I was blessed with a son, and then shortly thereafter, we flew to Mexico to bring my wife's older daughter to the United States, making us a family of five.

The ghosts of my past kept coming back. I dressed up in private so I could express my female self, but then my self-worth would plummet and I would dive back into working long hours because it was the only thing that made me happy; it was the only thing I thought I was good at.

Logicware and Contraband

When I left Interplay, a gentleman I was doing hardware projects with suggested we go into business together. As with Interplay, I really wasn't interested in the "business side" of running a company. Since that was his field, I agreed and we formed Logicware. Since I was sick of the games business, we started with a project where I programmed Laserdisc recorders for an amusement park experience. But that project fell apart when the client ran out of money, so I had to face the question of what to do next. Asking myself that question, I realized: games were my life. So, I obtained a contract and started doing game ports again. As with Interplay, it was a challenge making payroll because I had to get the games out before I would get paid and be able to sign my employees' paychecks.

However, my business partner ended up alienating much of the studio, leading a group to quit and form a rival studio. Later, the rest of us parted ways *en masse* and let Logicware collapse. Those of us who were left formed

Contraband Entertainment. This was the first company in which I took the role of chief executive officer (CEO), despite my lack of formal training.

However, by this time it was the early 2000s, and the dot-com bust eventually took us out. The companies we were doing business with shut down and stopped hiring us, and I had the unenviable job of laying off my friends. I locked myself in a room and cried for an hour over my failure to keep them employed. A small number volunteered to stay with the firm, despite not getting paid, in the hopes we'd get a new contract and get us back on payroll.

I changed again at that time. I had always considered those I worked with as co-workers, not employees. I had treated them like family, the family I wished I had when I was small, who cared for each other and watched each other's backs—180 degrees different than my job at Interplay, where backstabbing, politics, and brown-nosing were the order of the day.

Living among men, being treated as a man, and seeing firsthand how little women were valued made me internally vow that I'd never stoop to that level. I would always treat everyone fairly and give them a voice, no matter who they were.

I renewed my efforts and landed the stripped-down Contraband Entertainment some cell phone game contracts which earned enough money that my friends could eat and pay rent and not much else. And then we got a juicy contract to help Electronic Arts out of a jam.

Electronic Arts and Being Reborn

I had learned a lot by this time. I had friends. People liked me. I had a family. I could get work for not just me, but for my friends. After we completed our work on *Medal of Honor: Rising Sun*, Electronic Arts made job offers for me and my team. I was flattered. Never had I been offered this much money for a salary. With my kids reaching high school, I decided that I needed some stability in my life, and after conferring with my friends, we decided to take the offer. I wound down Contraband and placed its assets into storage.

After a few weeks of working at Electronic Arts (EA), a dam burst in my mind. I had spent so much of my life burying myself in my work, my companies, and my family that I had never spent time dealing with me.

I had a secret.

Something that my family knew, but no one else did.

It had to come out, and it was time.

I fell into a deep depression. It was 2003. I had seen what the game industry had done to other women like me, and it was not good. I had to get help, so I reached out to a therapist near where I lived and after one session he told me, "I can't help you, but I know someone who can." He gave me the phone number to the Los Angeles Gender Center. I hesitated, because I knew what that meant; I was terrified to blow my cover. But my true identity was already leaking out. I was getting comments like, "You're not like the other guys," and "Are you gay?" Each time, it struck fear in my soul: How did they know?

After three months of intense therapy, I could finally admit what I was: a woman, hiding in a man's body, enjoying male privilege, living in a world that was neither male nor female. I made the decision and began on my path to unmask my true self.

I was so terrified about being found out that I hacked EA's network, to read the human resources (HR) files on transgenderism, expecting that even the act of accessing the files using my company account would get me terminated. Imagine my joy at finding that the employee policy was recently updated to make it a terminating offense to discriminate *against* people undergoing a gender transition. I promptly contacted HR, and then my manager, and we made a plan for my transition.

To say my announcement was a nonevent is an understatement. Some may think Electronic Arts is "Evil Incarnate," but the people there welcomed me with open arms. My favorite response was "So, you're a chick. Does it affect your work? If not, get back to it."

However, as the years went by, I noticed that people treated me different than when they had thought I was male. My opinion stopped mattering. My input was ignored. My coding skills were dismissed. Only when I explained that I once used a nom de plume and was the programmer of many hit games was my competence accepted, but with reservations. Somehow, by my having a female name, the perception of my IQ had dropped by 40 points overnight. There even was a game at EA called "Guess Becky's job," where new employees were brought to my hexicle (a six-sided cubicle) and asked what my job was. Even though my office was filled with computers, development kits, and screens full of source code, I was called "User Interface Designer," "Audio Designer," "Tech Artist," and even "Office Manager." Being female automatically made it hard for anyone to guess I was a programmer.

I had to do something about this. We have to do something about this. Once, people would have assumed their doctor would be male, or their dentist, or a judge. Today, all three fields have prominent and respected women in them.

I am a programmer. I created many classic video games. I am a woman.

Endnotes

1. Clance, Pauline Rose, and Imes, Suzanne. "The Imposter Phenomenon in High-Achieving Women: Dynamics and Therapeutic Intervention." *Psychotherapy Theory, Research and Practice.* Fall 1978.
2. Dore, Madeline. "How to Conquer Imposter Syndrome." *Arts Hub.* 27 Jul 2015. Available at http://www.artshub.com.au/news-article/career-advice/professional-development/madeleine-dore/how-to-conquer-impostor-syndrome-248804?utm_source=ArtsHub+Australia&utm_campaign=e499ec7752-UA-828966-1&utm_medium=email&utm_term=0_2a8ea75e81-e499ec7752-304031305
3. Mohr, Tara Sophia. "Why Women Don't Apply for Jobs Unless They're 100% Qualified." *Harvard Business Review.* 25 Aug 2014. Available at https://hbr.org/2014/08/why-women-dont-apply-for-jobs-unless-theyre-100-qualified

4

From the Beginning

Frequently when someone objects to making video games more friendly to female players or developers, they accuse women of being "interlopers" or even "cultural colonialists,"[1] who are somehow moving into areas of the game industry and Internet that are natively occupied only by men. "But gaming has always been by men, for men," is a common argument. Or "games are the last place a man can be a man."

If this book does nothing else, we hope it shows the lie behind such statements. Women have been an essential part of gaming from the very beginning. Polygon's Tracey Lien wrote a fascinating piece, "No Girls Allowed," which showcases how deliberate marketing decisions changed video games into a "toy for boys" instead of a pastime that was seen as largely gender neutral prior to 1983.

> … marketing is so powerful that it can shape our values and beliefs, and we're often not even aware that it's happening. Coca-Cola's marketing campaigns in the 1920s are the reason why the modern-day image of Santa Claus is a jovial, plump man in a Coca-Cola Red suit. Prior to Coca-Cola, there was no consistent image of Santa. He was often represented as a skinny man who sometimes wore green and sometimes wore brown. So if Coca-Cola could sell us the modern-day Santa, the game industry would not have had much trouble selling the idea that video games are for males.

The entire article[2] is well worth reading, but the short version is that in 1983, the game industry experienced a 97% drop in sales that nearly wiped out the future of video games. When Nintendo revived the industry, they did so by marketing heavily to boys. In the 1990s, as those boys grew up, M-rated (and usually violent) video games became the norm, marketing heavily to boys and men. Before those deliberate campaigns, many early video game ads featured boys and girls equally, and most early titles were nonviolent, gender-neutral games like *Pong* (1972), *3D Tic-Tac-Toe* (1979), or even *Tetris* (1989).

On the development side, women were also present. In addition to some of the women in this book whose careers started in the 1980s, the early history of video games includes many important female developers. The first one many people think of is industry legend Roberta Williams, designer of the groundbreaking *Mystery House*, co-founder of powerhouse 1980s developer Sierra, and the originator of the graphical adventure game genre. Williams's incredible accomplishments assured her a place in Computer Gaming World's Hall of Fame.[3]

Other, less celebrated early pioneers include

- Carol Shaw, who designed and programmed the aforementioned *3D Tic-Tac-Toe* (1979) for Atari, and *River Raid* (1982) for Activision
- Dona Bailey, who co-created and designed the arcade classic *Centipede* (1981)
- Ann Westfall, co-founder of Free Fall Associates, the first third-party developer for Electronic Arts, and programmer of the hit game *Archon* (1983)
- Jane Jenson, Roberta Williams's successor in the adventure game genre, designer and writer of the *Gabriel Knight* (1993) series, among others
- Amy Briggs, who in 1983 wrote the first American romance adventure game for girls, *Plundered Hearts*[4]
- Reiko Kodama, a character artist at Sega who started on titles like *Ninja Princess* (1984) and went on to be the executive designer on *Phantasy Star* (1989)
- Yoko Shimomura, who composed the soundtracks of *Street Fighter II* (1991), *Kingdom Hearts* (2002), and many others
- Corinne Yu, programmer on *King's Quest* (1984), *Anachronix* (2001), and many others

Despite the more even-handed marketing of the early days, video game development was still a male-dominated field, and these women did face sexism in the workplace. Carol Shaw recalls a memorable incident in which Ray Kassar, the president of Atari, first met her and said, "Oh, at last! We have a female game designer. She can do cosmetics color matching and interior decorating cartridges!" Fortunately, her fellow designers knew better and advised her to ignore him.[5]

In the 1980s and 1990s, a flood of new, talented women joined the industry, including our own Brenda Romero (Chapter 2), Sheri Graner Ray (Chapter 18), and Megan Gaiser (Chapter 20). Since the explosion of the Nintendo Entertainment System onto the market in 1983, two and a half generations have grown up with the constant presence of a game console (and eventually mobile gaming device) in their homes. Despite the pervasive marketing to boys, many of those boys had sisters, female friends, and eventually daughters who saw what was happening on screen and wanted in on the action. And that rise in interest has been mirrored in development teams, in which the percentage of women has risen to nearly a quarter (22%) in 2014, roughly double the 11.5% of teams which were female in 2009.[6]

And this representation is important! With more than twice as many adult women actively playing games now than boys under 18,[7] it is crucial that the industry respond to these changing demographics by embracing the women who have always been there in the trenches, trying to make the kinds of games they loved.

Endnotes

1. Slater, Tom, "The Year of the Cultural Colonialist." *Free Speech Now, a Spiked Project.* 23 Dec 2014. Available at http://www.spiked-online.com/freespeechnow/fsn_article/the-year-of-the-cultural-colonialist#.VS2SL5MYOYE
2. Lien, Tracey, "No Girls Allowed." *Polygon.* 2 Dec 2013. Available at http://www.polygon.com/features/2013/12/2/5143856/no-girls-allowed
3. "Hall of Fame," *Computer Gaming World.* 23 Mar 2005. Available at http://www.1up.com/features/hall-of-fame?pager.offset=0
4. Cohen, D.S. "The Most Important Women in the History of Videogames." *About Tech.* 2015. Available at http://classicgames.about.com/od/history/tp/HistoricWomeninClassicGames.htm
5. Edwards, Benji. "Interview: Carol Shaw, the First Female Game Developer." *Vintage Computing and Gaming.* 12 Oct 2011. Available at http://www.vintagecomputing.com/index.php/archives/800
6. Makuch, Eddie. "Percentage of Female Developers Has More Than Doubled Since 2009." *Gamespot.* 24 Jun 2014. Available at http://www.gamespot.com/articles/percentage-of-female-developers-has-more-than-doubled-since-2009/1100-6420680/
7. Sullivan, Gail. "Study: More Women Than Teenage Boys Are Gamers." *The Washington Post.* 22 Aug 2014. Available at http://www.washingtonpost.com/news/morning-mix/wp/2014/08/22/adult-women-gamers-outnumber-teenage-boys/

5

Judy Tyrer

Then and Now: Joining the Game Industry at an "Advanced" Age

Engineer: *Rainbow Six: Lockdown, Ghost Recon: Advanced Warfighter 1&2, Magic the Gathering: Tactics, Second Life, Selling: The Psychological Approach, Patient Management Simulator, Critical Strike Air Force Simulator*

Founder: 3 Turn Productions (*Ever, Jane*)

In March 2004, CNN wrote an article that advised job seekers to go to India. We in the computer industry had begun referring to this time as www. yourjobhasgonetoindia.com days. One programmer in my morning coffee klatch, before we all hit the pavement to look for no longer existent work, ended up taking a job as a greeter at Walmart because, "I have a mortgage to pay."

My son was 15 and we were discussing his future. I told him, "As much as you love to game, if I were you, I'd go into the video game industry." It was a definite "AHA!" moment. A little voice in the back of my head said, "You love to game, too. You could join the video game industry." But I was 50 and female, two very big strikes against me.

I discussed this choice with my sister, who gave me the most valuable advice ever. "You are not a statistic." And with that advice I chose to enter, for the second time as it turns out, the video game industry. I attended E3. I scoured the Internet for how to break in. I found Tom Sloper's[1] website and since he was local to me at the time, contacted him. He agreed to meet me. I bought him lunch and he advised me on what I would need. He felt that a demo would be the best way to show how my skills would transfer from distributed UNIX OS to gaming. He told me to look up the job titles and find the one that fit me best. As I had experience ripping apart Transmission Control Protocol/Internet Protocol (TCP/IP) packets to redirect traffic (shhh, don't tell—we're not supposed to do that), I thought network engineer was the title that best fit my skills.

At the same time, I learned how resumes needed to be worded to get traction. As I mention above, this was my second venture into video games. However, my first venture wasn't called video games; it was "Computer-Based Education." My very first post-degree job was at Control Data Corporation doing "Serious Games." When I moved the games I had published to the top of my resume, I suddenly started getting interviews, lots of them.

Sadly I did not yet have the skillset many companies wanted for gameplay programming, but with each interview I was given additional advice. And I began designing my demo—a biome simulation that would run a spawn table for a massively multiplayer online (MMO) game. It was built on the concept of minimizing bandwidth by sending deltas of data; I avoided the need for ACKs by sending three deltas at a time, etc. I wanted to show different problem-solving skills for the basic issue of managing bandwidth.

In the course of writing the demo, I wanted to know whether games push or pull from the server and so I wrote a question in the International Game Developers Association (IGDA) forums explaining the pros and cons of each approach and asking what was normally used. The response I received was "Send me your resume." After a few interviews and a cross-country move with teenagers (not highly recommended as they will whine for months about how you ruined their lives), I entered the video game industry as a network engineer for Ubisoft. I worked for them for the next 6 years until I was caught in a 25% head-count reduction.

A Good Cover Letter Goes Far

At this point, I wanted to start my own studio, but was not yet financially in a position to do so and unemployment required that I interview a minimum of twice a week. Having already incorporated my company, I took that task with a grain of salt by applying to senior design positions I knew I would not qualify for. And then I saw an ad that triggered my tirade on "all that is wrong with software development in the game industry."

As I read the cover letter I worried it was a bit too strong, but decided I didn't really want the job anyway, I wanted to build my own studio. So I submitted it.

I got a call from Sony Denver within 24 hours. The Director of Development's first words were, "I loved your cover letter." A few weeks later, I was off to Denver to pull the team together and ship *Magic The Gathering: Tactics* as lead engineer. I was very excited to bring my management skills to game development and combine them with what I had learned at Ubisoft.

We launched in time to meet our contractual obligations, although everyone on the team was a bit disappointed in the quality. But it was an excellent experience in setting priorities and cutting features in order to make a launch. I won't say it was the most fun I've ever had, and I highly recommend *not* trying to do a 36-hour launch in which no one on the team gets to sleep, but we did it.

And then SOE decided to consolidate its studios and, three weeks after closing on our home in the mountains, I was informed I was being transferred to San Diego, where instead of being lead engineer of the studio, I would be relegated to fixing I18N bugs in Flash. At that point in my life, this was not the direction I wanted my career to go in.

However, we still had debt from our move to Colorado (as the industry had changed from paying full moving costs to a set allowance, which was insufficient for a family of four). And so I embarked on what we considered "the least bad option" available.

The Year of Living with Uncertainty

I moved to San Francisco, leaving my family behind, and took a job as Senior Engineering Manager at Linden Lab working on *Second Life*. I would easily classify this year as one of the best possible years I could have had professionally, while everything in my private life was horrid because I was away from my family.

When we started what I later called "the year of living with uncertainty," it really was great fun. I had planned on making more frequent trips home, but I found that altitude plays a bigger role in living in the mountains than I had planned on. The altitude adjustment made coming home just for the weekend impossible.

At Linden Lab, my team ran 650K simulations on 10K servers and I was given an opportunity to play with server scale at a level very few have. I honestly believe this was the perfect opportunity to lead me to building my own game.

As the year wound to a close and I hit 59 ½, the time had come. Both of my children had independently decided to move home and there was no way I was going to live in San Francisco with my entire family in Colorado. I also had the unfortunate experience of driving myself to the emergency room with appendicitis. During that drive, I determined it was time to come home. Living away from my family was fun for about 9 months, and then it grew exceedingly old.

Live Where You Work and Work Where You Live

The first thing I did upon returning home was write my one and only blog post (to date, I expect to write more). It was on the value of remote work. "Live where you work and work where you live" became a fundamental cornerstone while building my studio, 3 Turn Productions.

And here we are, a successful Kickstarter campaign and 3 ½ years later, wrapping up the final feature of the game and moving into optimization and polish on *Ever, Jane: The Virtual World of Jane Austen*.

With launch six months away, it is tempting to focus completely on the game, but it is equally important to me to build the studio I want to build. It will be a combination of Locus Computing Corporation and Linden Lab, as they were the two best companies I've worked for.

I would dearly love to build a studio with a 0% attrition rate, but I realize that is unrealistic. Already I cannot compete with tootling round Europe in an RV and so I will be losing my community manager shortly after launch.

But I still believe ardently and adamantly in taking care of the people who work for me, the same way I was taken care of by those two companies. If you take care of your people, your people will take care of your product.

That has been my experience as a manager. I expect it to play out the same way now that I am CEO.

Promotional Art for Ever, Jane: The Virtual World of Jane Austen.
3 Turn Productions, Upcoming 2016

Problems in the Game Industry

The game industry differs from the early days of the computer industry in significant ways, but many of the issues of being a woman in a male-dominated field are similar. When I joined the computer industry, there were 10 jobs for every qualified person and so programmers were treated with a level of respect that we don't see in gaming. The early computer industry acknowledged how the brain works (and that some days it doesn't!), while the game industry tries to run more like manufacturing. For artists maybe this works more easily, as one can compare how long it takes one artist to model and texture a chair versus the time for another artist, and so the time to complete art assets can be more clearly estimated.

But for some reason the industry has been highly resistant to learning what the computer industry could teach about programming. Much of the process work I had done was thrown out the window. The argument was always, "we cannot use traditional software processes, because it has to be fun." I think the lack of process was the most shocking change, though the introduction of Scrum at least gave studios something to work with. I have an entire book in the works providing a new process I believe will improve production, at least for those doing the work. It is called Fuzzy Development and is loosely based on Fuzzy Logic.

Imposter Syndrome

But the similarities are still significant. One issue that was true then, though not yet labeled, was "Imposter Syndrome," and this hit me harder than many. Unlike most of my colleagues who had degrees in computer science, my degree was in English Literature and Secondary Education (with a minor in Geology). They knew UNIX inside and out and I was still learning. Many of them had always intended to have careers in programming, while I was told, "Learn to type, become a secretary and meet a nice young executive." (Thanks, Dad!)

While I was still a junior member of the technical staff, my lack of knowledge didn't bother me, but over time I got promoted and when I reached the title "Principal Member of the Technical Staff," I became increasingly worried by it.

It was at this point one of the best managers I have ever worked for gave me the best advice I've ever received. His name is Joel Lilienkamp and he later became my mentor, because I did my best work while working for him. He taught me the importance of good management.

Joel told me, "The only difference between you and Joe is that Joe knows if he doesn't know the answer he can look it up and you seem to think he just knows everything." It was so true. It never occurred to me that Joe spent as much time looking things up as I did. This was the first time we ever addressed "imposter syndrome," but it was a crucial one for me. Since then technology has exploded to the point that no one can know everything, so that has been a huge boon to those of us still suffering from this syndrome.

A History of Harassment

The other issue that gaming and the computer industry have in common is sexual harassment. Because I am of an older generation and was so happy just to have a foot in the corporate door, I tended to overlook what, in retrospect, was definitely harassment. I was just so thrilled to be at the party that I didn't care. I didn't care when, on a trip to Chicago, my male colleague said, "Don't tell my wife but I've been fantasizing about you ever since I heard we were going on this trip together. I was hoping for adjoining rooms." I didn't care when a year later the same colleague said, "My wife is 8 months pregnant. Can we get a hotel room? I'm desperate." Sexual harassment just was not discussed much back then.

But as Monica Lewinsky and Bill Clinton started to dominate the headlines, I became a bit less oblivious when my boss asked me late on a Friday night, "Why are you going home? Do you love your husband more than me?" I was transferred the following Monday. I mentioned the conversation to my supervisor, whose response was, "Who do you want to work for?" That was easy and I transferred once again to work for Joel.

The issue of harassment came to a head for me when color monitors were introduced and a large 36-inch monitor was put in the lab. My first introduction to the monitor was a tied-down, spread-eagle crotch shot with whips in the picture. *Beyond* inappropriate for work. I protested and I learned quickly who my friends were not. In retaliation for my getting porn banned from the company, my team—all colleagues I considered good friends—chose to have the wrap party for the project at a local strip bar, knowing it would offend me and I would not attend.

Screenshot from Ever, Jane: The Virtual World of Jane Austen, *3 Turn Productions, Upcoming 2016*

Of all the issues I had to deal with as the only woman in the room, that was the hardest and most painful. The truth is that boy's clubs really don't want girls included and that is one of the most challenging issues we face.

Endnote

1. Tom Sloper is a long-time game developer and creative director at Activision and other companies.

6

Brianna Wu

Founder: Giant Spacekat

Head of Development: *Revolution 60*

Co-Host: *Isometric, Rocket*

Growing up in the poorest state in America, Mississippi, I was extremely lucky to have what so few did: opportunity.

As a child I was always looking for something to learn, a way to challenge myself into being something I wasn't supposed to be. When my mother bought a computer for our home (practically unheard of where I lived), I immersed myself in it and learned everything I could about the hardware and software.

As a teen, I decided to take my knowledge a step further and registered for college classes to learn programming. Shortly after, I dropped out of the class, stunned to realize that I had somehow already managed to teach myself the basics, setting myself up for a career I didn't realize was on the horizon.

After college, I got my entrepreneurial feet wet by starting my own animation company. It was unsuccessful, and when that path abruptly ended, I floundered a little. Sick of, and more than a little wary of, what Mississippi had to offer, I packed my car and drove to DC. I was intent on getting a job in politics. Wanting to impact change.

That metaphorical and physical drive is part of what defines me. I look around and want something different. Want to step away from something that didn't work, and try something else. I decide I want it, and I make it happen. That's what I do, every day.

I've ended up in so many different fields: working as a journalist, dabbling as a teen in the frowned-upon art of fake IDs. But underneath it all was gaming. When I was up, I played games with friends and for fun. When I was down, I played to pass the time and ease the pain.

Eventually, life turned a new corner, I met and married my husband Frank. I followed him to Boston, where we had an opportunity too good to turn down. A relative let us fix up her house, and then live in it for free. Looking back, I remember the elbows-deep disgusting mess we got ourselves into—stripping asbestos and scraping wallpaper until we turned it into something livable. But the money we saved gave us the startup funds we needed to create something amazing—Giant Spacekat, my development studio, creators of *Revolution 60* and *Cupcake Crisis*.

Promotional Art for Revolution 60,
Giant Spacekat, 2015

I'm not going to lie, I love my job and I love my colleagues, but working in games is the advanced mode of being a woman in tech. Welcome to hard mode: No Items, Fox Only, Final Destination.

Choose Your Stage

Why is it so tough for women in games? For starters, this is an industry that has been marketed as a space for men for over 30 years. As mentioned, in 1985, Nintendo was bringing the Nintendo Entertainment System (NES) to market, and made a conscious choice to market it to boys between five and ten years old. When the SNES came out, they expanded that to boys between five and fifteen.

If you look at the marketing materials for Nintendo in the mid-1980s, they almost always assumed the player was male. From sexualized ads for Konami titles, to posters in *Nintendo Power* encouraging boys to be Captain Commando, there was little inclusion of women when representing gamers and game developers. Case in point: Nintendo's famous animated series *Captain N: The Game Master* stars a young boy who is sucked into a world of video games. The main female character in Captain N is a princess who wears a midriff top and is frequently a damsel in distress.

This choice in Nintendo's marketing had huge repercussions for who played video games. According to *Variety*, in 1989, only 3% of gamers were female.[1] And that lack of players also had ramifications for who chose to go into video games as a career.

The second major factor behind the lack of women in games is blatant (if unconscious) sexism by male professionals in this field. It's everywhere. Take it from me, the game industry is filled with men who believe they are too smart to be sexist. They take pride in being "open-minded," and are fine with women in theory, but they're very hesitant to reflect on their actions and understand the things that colleagues and companies do that can push us away.

A Sexist Status Quo

Look at AAA development. Note who has the senior positions in art, programming, level design, animation, and sound. They are almost never women. Look at our journalistic institutions. Out of *Game Informer's*

18 current editors, 17 are men. *Giant Bomb* employs no women or minorities whatsoever. *IGN* has privately been described to me as "a frat house," by women who have worked there.

There's a pattern I've seen over and over in my career. When I talk to men one-on-one, they privately tell me how much they want to see more women in this field. They position themselves as an ally, and tell me how much they want it to get better. But they're rarely able to accept a critique of things *they've* done that hurt women. Any kind of criticism, no matter how carefully worded, and the conversation gets defensive very quickly.

As a result, our industry has been very slow to change with the times. More days than not, the gender assumptions in game development are stuck in the 1980s.

When I think about the game industry, I often conjure up a mental image of the Twitch TV offices, which they were generous enough to let me tour this year. Everywhere I looked, there were Nerf toys, male action figures on desks, comic books, and all the accoutrement of boys who had not quite grown up. It's a good representation of what the game industry has become—an entire business built in the image of a very particular person.

It's a system that must be bliss for the Peter Pans, some of whom are in their thirties and forties by now, but it's not a system that spends much time thinking about the rest of us. Game development is full of men who mean well, but lack a perspective about how the rest of us experience the world.

A New Challenger Appears

That said, things are improving. Most men are aware things aren't great for women in games, and want it to get better. Everything about the current direction of the industry suggests that it's *going* to get better.

For starters, the number of women playing games is positively exploding. In 2007, women were 17% of the market. And, as of the last study I read, women are now 52% of the video game market![2] In 2015, the average gamer is now a 36-year-old woman! The game industry, like all businesses, is ultimately about money. And the reality is, men are no longer the primary way companies earn their money.

The second factor is the huge increase in public awareness of what women are facing in the game industry. This hasn't happened serendipitously.

Brave women in this field have put it all on the line, flagging problems and putting public pressure on the major players. And it's working. I have heard more conversations in 2015 about hiring practices than in any other year.

Bottom line, if you are a woman in games, a woman who *wants* to be in games, or a woman who loves games, games need you. I need you, and my friends need you. For far too long, games have been a boy's club. We're getting so close to having a critical mass of women in game development, a number where we can't be ignored.

We're so close to winning the game, but we can't do it without you.

You're Fine Just the Way That You Are

So often, when we discuss women in tech, there seems to be an assumption that we need to adapt who we are or how we present ourselves. Be more confident! Be nicer! Be more laid back! There's this assumption that there's a "right" path that will shelter us from the worst excesses.

This is flat out wrong. I want to tell you right now, if you are a woman reading this—you're fine the way that you are. There is no single right way to be a woman in tech!

Looking at my female friends in the field, we run the gamut of ages, personalities, career specialties, and career tactics. I have friends who are firebrand editors, introverted engineers, outspoken feminists, women who are uncomfortable getting involved in gender issues, sex-positive writers, bubbly video hosts, and women with no filter whatsoever. None of them are doing "women in games" wrong.

Whoever you are, you have a place here. You don't need to change, the industry does.

I know women who have endured serious sexual harassment, women who have faced gender-based discrimination, women who have had to leave jobs because of sexist environments. But, I also have a lot of friends who *haven't* experienced these things. We all have horror stories of guys acting like jerks, but the worst excesses are doled out almost at random. Roll a die, because there's no way to determine what your career will bring.

I can say, I have experienced the absolute worst harassment a person can experience, and I'm still here. I love my job, and I love the game industry. If you really want to work in games—you can get through it, I promise.

Getting in the Door

Being in charge of hiring at my company, I see a lot of resumes. So, if you're reading this book with a desire to get into the game industry, I want to give some practical advice about getting your foot in the door.

First, employers hire people in order to solve problems. Liking video games is not a skill. Having ideas is not a skill. You need to be incredibly good at something. The game industry has so many subspecialties, so find something you're passionate about and get obsessed with it until you're really fantastic.

When I was starting, I decided I wanted to learn texturing. And I spent a lot of what I call, "butt-in-chair time." There's no substitute for butt-in-chair time. It's where you tinker, solve, fail, and learn until you can do something at a professional level. The video game industry generally cares about your portfolio much more than any degree.

Speaking of college, I have seen a lot of kids robbed of $200,000, who seem to have graduated without any marketable skills or portfolio. Undoubtedly, professional education has value—particularly in something like animation. But, if you go down this path, don't be fooled into thinking your degree will guarantee you a job. You're going to be competing with people with years of experience for every job—developing a portfolio is everything.

If you're just starting, here are some areas I would suggest not specializing in: music composition, concept art, game writing, and voice acting. It's not that you can't make a career in these areas, it's that they are glutted with people looking to get their foot in the door, with very few available positions.

Specialties I would strongly suggest going into would be: zBrush, C++, C#, material creation, lighting specialist, VFX specialist, technical rigging, and OpenGL. These are technical skills that have a high value in a game production pipeline. They can't be easily outsourced, and they're mission critical for shipping a professional game.

Increasingly, as indies take a larger and larger market share, being a generalist is going to have value. I would consider myself a generalist with three subspecialties, which is helpful for running a studio. But, if your mission is to work in AAA, you need a double T-shaped resume—meaning you have two areas of deep specialty.

And if you're hoping to go into game marketing, the one thing you inarguably need are connections. Marketing is a critical part of shipping a successful game. But a love for social media does not make you a marketer.

The best marketers have a lot of connections, and are amazing at networking. Being able to compose a Tweet is not a particularly impressive job skill. If you want to compete at the pro level, you need to start developing connections today.

Confidence Is Everything

The strangest phenomenon I've seen in my career is this: all the women I know who are amazing at their jobs never think that they are.

I have a friend who's easily one of the best games journalists in the entire business, and yet every time I hang out with her she seems plagued by self-doubt. Meanwhile, her drastically less-talented male cohorts are doing mediocre work and rarely seem to harbor these same nagging worries. It's truly bizarre.

Overconfidence is unattractive and easy to spot in any gender. But believing in myself is never something I've regretted. This business is always changing. The next game I'm doing involves technology I've never used … but I'm certain when I sit down I'll get it done. By trusting in myself, I inspire that same confidence in my team and the people around me.

It's especially important to have self-confidence when dealing with men. Remember, unconscious sexism causes them to assume men are competent until proven otherwise, and women are incompetent until proven otherwise. When I meet someone in this field for the first time, I make a point to use language and jargon that communicate that I am a software engineer … which stops people from assuming I work in marketing.

It is never rude to ask for the same respect you give.

Pick Your Partners Carefully

I cannot communicate how important this is. Picking your partners is critical for any business relationship. But for women in this field, getting into a bad business arrangement can ruin everything. Every time I have ever overridden my instincts with logic, it has proven to be a mistake.

Because, the truth is, this is a field with a lot of men who mean well, but are sexist in ways they don't understand. Intellectually, they believe women should be able to work in this field just as any man can. But, unconsciously, they have a lot of gendered assumptions that can undermine the work you're doing together.

For example, I once had a working arrangement with someone who wanted more women to work in game development. But, he was the worst mansplainer[3] I have ever worked with in my professional career. Any point I made, he thought he knew better. And any time we disagreed, he grew hostile very quickly.

This is what researchers call "unconscious sexism." Subconsciously, this person assumed he should be in charge, assumed he knew more, and grew uncomfortable when I challenged him. And this behavior is absolutely everywhere in this field. It doesn't help that Peter Pan syndrome is so prevalent in our field—a lot of men in game development have an unconscious and very adolescent resentment of women.

There are many ways to deal with unconscious sexists. I have a friend who leverages "relentless niceness," being incredibly pleasant even when she's internally screaming. I have some friends who deal with it by remaining very closed off with people by default, not letting many people into their inner circle. For me, I handle it by being open, honest, and direct. The point is, if you are a woman in games, you're undoubtedly going to run into men like this, and you don't want to build your most important working relationships out of them.

There is no universal answer to unconscious sexism. Every woman has to search within herself, figure out what feels natural to her, and learn to use it strategically.

Network Lag

It's impossible to overstate the value of networking. For me, as a woman who runs a company, the majority of my time is spent taking meetings, giving and asking for favors, helping connect people, doing press and a thousand other social interactions that get me the resources to achieve my goals.

Very few people, especially on the technical side, like networking. But it has to be done—and let's face it, women are at a huge disadvantage.

I'll tell you a story. I have a friend who works for a major institution in games. She was the first woman hired there, and they threw a huge bash a few weeks after she was brought on. The pictures were all over their social media—dudes getting trashed, dancing with random girls at the bar, playing video games at their office. The entire evening was straight out of *Animal House*.

And they forgot to invite the one woman who worked there, the one they had just hired. She confronted her manager about it afterward, and he was genuinely confused. "I totally forgot you worked here!" he said.

Which is a pretty perfect metaphor for being a woman in games.

Personally, I have found limited value to networking in the bar and party scene. I concentrate on lunches out with people, Twitter interactions, and professional events like PAX. I spent a lot of time asking myself where I need to go, then working on connections around that goal.

The truth is, game developers do change jobs relatively frequently. And if you want to have a long-term career, you can't neglect building a strong network of connections.

You Have to Have Girlfriends

I've often thought about doing a game called, "Woman in Tech." The idea is: there are a thousand things that happen every day that sap your energy and health. And the only thing that heals that damage are friendships with other women.

Put bluntly, there is no way you will survive in this field without female friends.

Friendship with other women isn't just about blowing off steam, talking about problems, or getting advice. Other women in the field will be your best opportunity for networking. I realize this is a very *Sisterhood of the Traveling Pants* thing for me to say, but I really think women in tech are all in this together. If we aren't there for each other, then we've lost the game.

I make it a point of professional pride to do all I can to promote the women around me. If I'm going to a party, I ask myself who would benefit if I bought them along. I encourage people to hire women I believe in, and even started two podcasts with the goal of promoting women I believe are worth hearing.

But … There Will Be Drama

I told a friend of mine I was writing this chapter, and asked her if she'd figured out how to avoid drama with other women. We were out to lunch, she buried her face in the tablecloth, and just muttered, "Arrrrrgggggghhhhhh."

As far as I can tell, some women in this field are so used to being the only girl at the party that they're flat out mean to other women. Some of us are damaged from our experiences, and divide everything into a Manichaean world of who can and cannot be trusted. Some of us are so invested in the careers we've built that we're just plain cruel to anyone who's not in our self-defined clubhouse.

Sadly, there is no way to avoid hostile interactions altogether. But, I do have tips for minimizing the impact.

I always try to build people up around me, even when there is nothing to gain. And even when I don't like another woman in this field, I keep that to myself. I try to show kindness to absolutely everyone I can. And I don't take sides, unless it's in private.

You will not please everyone. Things you do and decisions you make will piss people off. All you can do is try to be reasonable. But, over a career, when you have a reputation for making reasonable decisions, it will pay off.

Lead characters from Revolution 60,
Giant Spacekat, 2015

Final Words

More than anything else, game development is a career where you build things. My best advice to anyone building something is to be pragmatic: relentlessly, ruthlessly pragmatic.

The technology of game development is always changing. The tools and platforms we're using today will not be the ones we're using in five years.

The turnover is high. This is a field where having a backup plan and being able to adapt are absolutely critical.

But if you're a woman in games right now, your unique perspective is what the industry desperately needs. Games are stagnated—the monoculture has lost the ability to innovate. And a new audience of women gamers thirsts for the kind of genuine experience you are uniquely able to make.

I won't tell you that it will be easy, but I can promise you it will be fun. I believe in you.

Endnotes

1. Grasser, Marc. "Videogame Biz: Women Still Very Much in the Minority." *Variety.* 1 Oct 2013. Available at http://variety.com/2013/digital/features/womengamers1200683299-1200683299/
2. Jayanth, Meg. "52% of Gamers Are Women—But the Industry Doesn't Know It." *The Guardian.* 18 Sep 2014. Available at http://www.theguardian.com/commentisfree/2014/sep/18/52-percent-people-playing-games-women-industry-doesnt-know
3. A man who re-explains things a woman is saying as if she couldn't understand them, or tries to explain things to a woman about a field she is an expert in.

7

Karisma Williams

Technical Artist: *Charlie and the Chocolate Factory, Stubbs the Zombie, Zathura, Prey, Bioshock, 50 Cent: BulletProof, Ghost Recon Advanced Warfare, Animales de la Muerte, Destroy All Humans 3: P.O.T.F., 1vs100*

UI/UX Designer: *Kinect Adventures, Kinect Star Wars, Battle Nations, MetalStorm First Strike*

As I held the controller, I concentrated on navigating *Donkey Kong* through the water level. I had never been here before but I was sure I would be able to beat this level. The hustle and bustle of various family downstairs felt miles away; my world was just me and my Super Nintendo. Five minutes earlier I had been told my mother had passed away. I was 12 years old.

Growing Up

Very early in my life, adversity became a common occurrence. So much that I feel uncomfortable when it's not a part of my process in anything I do. My mother was integral to building the foundation of who I would become. Education was very important to her.

She would say that people can take everything else away from you, but they can never take your education. Growing up poor, she was aware of how important education was and made sure my brother and I had the best opportunities to learn. My father was a bit more distant, but worked for IBM for 25 years. He often brought home computers, and introduced console gaming to me when he brought home a Nintendo Entertainment System bundle complete with Zapper Gun and Mat.

I grew up in Chicago, Illinois, in one of the most historic and diverse neighborhoods in the country: Hyde Park. Being part of the University of Chicago campus, the neighborhood's diversity was easy to see. President Obama—who was a senator at the time—spoke at my high school graduation. At the same time, like in any big city one is simply a bus ride away from some of the most dangerous neighborhoods. I had friends from all walks of life and nationalities. Despite being African American, I never felt like a minority. Growing up without a mother, I had very little female influence in my life.

Most of my good friends were guys, and my hobbies at the time (including basketball and teaching myself programming) helped further that. I'm not one to share a lot about myself, but I know it is key to understanding how I saw the game industry. Games are an escape for many people. For me games were an alternative. Games were there to keep an overactive mind busy instead of getting me in trouble. To this day, I credit gaming with keeping me on a path. I don't know the moment when I decided I wanted to make games for a living, but it was definitely before college. During college, I made sure every free assignment related in some way to gaming. This was the beginning of my hyper-focus on breaking into the industry.

Determined to Break In

I graduated in four years with two bachelor degrees. I knew it would mean nothing in the industry I wanted to be in. I put in late nights for months with my good friend Adversity trying to crack the industry code. This was before the days of LinkedIn, and at the time I didn't realize it but being a double minority—African American and a woman—only stacked the odds against me. The industry to this day is all about networking. I am sure back then companies were even less diverse than now. Most white male game developers don't run in the same circles as African American women from Chicago. So, how would I ever break in?

The Internet.

The Internet allows you to be whomever you want. At a very early age, I had my own identity online. My alias did not denote my gender, race, or age. It allowed me to cross over barriers I could not in real life. Without saying anything, you are assumed to be male and most likely white. I was able to meet someone online who believed in my ambition, which led to my very first job in the industry. When I was frustrated at the struggle and felt my accomplishments had been dismissed, this mentor told me something that stuck with me throughout my career. "Get used to it, you will always have to prove yourself …"

I experienced my first layoff at my first job in my twenties. My father was shocked. He had worked in a time where you had a job for life if you wanted it. He had taken an early retirement with a pension from IBM after 25 years. Compared to that, the instability of the game industry was monumental; layoffs were as common as a thunderstorm. But it was only as big a deal as you made it. Each time I lost a job, I believed in myself and I went on to bigger and better things.

My first jobs were at smaller and mid-size companies. There was rarely anyone like me there. Being surrounded by men was not a discomfort to me. If anything, it felt comfortable, as that was how I grew up. I had more men help me in my career than women. I understood men; women not so much. I also noticed there were very few minorities in the industry, men or women.

As time went on, I ended up at the top-tier gaming companies in the industry; namely Valve Corporation and Microsoft, the latter of which is where I have spent the majority of my career to date. By the time I was in my late twenties, I was at Microsoft and had shipped 10+ games on various platforms. As I looked around, it was the same story as at many of the smaller game companies. Very little diversity. I had finally made it, but it was bittersweet. My mother wasn't there to see it. And once the rush was over of breaking in and reaching my goal despite the naysayers, I could not help but look around and feel lonely. There was no one to relate to. No one like me.

Be the Best at What You Do

In high school one of my mentors told me, "You will be the very best at whatever you choose to do or you will end up in jail." What he meant was even if I chose to do something illegal, I would be so good at it that I would end up on the police radar and thus in jail.

I had a gift that was like clay that I could mold into whatever I wanted. Right before I graduated college, this mentor died in an accident. His funeral was the first and last funeral I attended after my mother's. His words never left me and each year as I got closer to my goals, he was proven right time and again.

My entire career philosophy has been based on my ability to be the very best at what I do. I naively assumed talent would overcome all ignorance and discrimination. I have been in conversations with director-level management that I know would not have happened had I been a different race or gender. I often wonder—given my accomplishments—if I was a white male, just how high would I be in any given corporate structure? One of the most interesting conversations I've had in my career was with the legal department for a well-known corporation. After reading the false accusations from many at the corporation, and looking at my accomplishments both internally and externally, the lawyer's only response was just how impressed he was with me. He couldn't say much more, but it helped me understand how big everything was.

Those who are not as talented will work very hard to control those who are. They will work very hard to keep things comfortable for themselves. Diversity doesn't benefit those already in control. You can't control something you don't understand and too many people don't understand those who are different from them. Different cultures and sexes have different ways of communicating, and when there are no policies to encourage people to understand instead of judge each other, the barriers continue to widen. I have spoken with many minorities in the game industry who are afraid to speak up during meetings, or afraid to show any emotion for fear it will be misinterpreted and lead to them losing their jobs. The point of having a diverse team is to have diverse views, so the end product will reach a wider audience. When the few diverse views in the room are stifled out of fear, the industry doesn't gain anything except a point on a data sheet somewhere.

I haven't focused on what my role was on any of my projects, because it doesn't matter. The hurdles I have overcome would have been there regardless of the job I did. The industry has been filled with more ups than downs for me, from shipping my first game, to being a part of the Kinect launch team which allowed people with disabilities to experience gaming in ways they couldn't before. My experience in the industry has shown me you can have a positive impact on others, and has given me the ability to motivate others. The people I've met in the industry are like family to me, and I am grateful for all the big brothers I have whom I will no doubt be in touch with for years to come.

"Confident" or "Arrogant"?

Game development is where I feel most at home. Everything just comes naturally to me. It is my domain, and I approach things within it with confidence. And being a woman displaying confidence in a field dominated by men gets you quickly written off as "arrogant."

Despite not doing more than any successful man is doing, you are labeled even by other women who are trying to fit in. Growing up, I was a huge fan of pro-wrestling. One of my favorites was Shawn Michaels, arguably one of the best performers of his time. A lot of his peers didn't

Crunch

Crunch is an issue that affects everyone in the game industry, not just women, though older developers and working parents often find it a harder burden to bear. "Crunch," sometimes called a "Death March," is the industry term for enforced overtime, often for months on end, with the goal of getting a game out to meet an unrealistic deadline.[1] This issue was first brought to public attention in 2004 by our own Erin Hoffman-John (Chapter 15), writing under the name of ea_spouse, who opened a conversation around Electronic Arts's illegal overtime, eventually leading EA to settle several class-action lawsuits for tens of millions of dollars.[2]

Yet a decade later, in the 2014 IGDA Developer Satisfaction Survey, 81% of respondents said they had experienced crunch within the last year, and 45% had experienced more than two periods of crunch within a single year. A full half of respondents reported that crunch was expected in their workplace as a normal part of the job. When asked for the reasons as to why crunch continues to happen so often, "Poor/unrealistic scheduling was the most frequent choice (53%), followed by feature creep (36%), unclear expectations (35%), insufficient staffing (31%) and inexperienced management (25%)."[3]

Since most game developers are paid an annual salary, rather than an hourly wage, these death march crunch periods are paid the same as a normal 40-hour work week, regardless of whether developers are expected to work 50, 60, or even 80 hours a week. And given the industry's incredibly high turnover rate, in which many companies staff up during production on a project, only to fire everyone the minute the game goes out the door,[4] often these long crunch periods—which can destroy a developer's mental and physical health and lead to divorce—are repaid with nothing more than a pink slip and another disheartening job search.

Editor

like him and his attitude was not the best, but no one disagreed about his talent and ability to perform and deliver each night. I am the very best at what I do. No one in the industry does what I can. No one can impact a product in the ways I can. I set a very high bar for myself and those I work with. The difference between pro-wrestling and the gaming industry is that many people in games are OK with mediocrity and being a part of it.

"You have to understand your bar is set much higher than others …," yet another mentor said to me as I sat in his office, furious about various issues at the studio. One thing I have learned is people will often misinterpret my passion for delivering high quality for being negative. Growing up with adversity by my side means I am very skeptical and quick to spot what could go wrong. I have learned through experience that when things are going right, there's no need to waste energy on it. At all times, my focus is on what can be improved.

I am not easily impressed by people with fancy titles talking fast and saying everything is fine, when I can read public financial reports myself. This is just a part of growing up in survival mode; you can trust no one but yourself. Those who know me well understand this; those who don't, get the wrong perception of my approach.

Managing people's perception of me was a new concept to me, one I never thought of until I was face-to-face with a senior director. That was when I was told it doesn't matter what you actually do; it's the perception of what others think you do. Where I am from, that just doesn't work. It's all about what you do. Period. Perception is often wrong, and will cost you your life in the wrong neighborhood. So why would a corporation base anything on people's perceptions? Why would a corporation continue to base decisions about people's careers on these perceptions even when proven wrong with actual data? Since we know it's human nature to have a more positive perception of people who are similar to you, what does this mean for diversity?

There are bigger things at play (mostly involving money, I would learn as time went on). At some point, everyone makes a choice in their career. You can focus on managing perception or actually doing. Perception can get tricky, as all it takes is one wrong move, even outside the company on social media, and you will find yourself too much trouble for any company to hire despite your capabilities. I have always chosen to focus on doing, to be so good they have no choice but to call you. Like Apple bringing back Steve Jobs, I believe no matter how companies act when at odds with talent, in the end everyone wants to "win" and they need talent to do so.

I mention these things because I want to be clear that none of the challenges, or people who attempted to block my career, have changed my view of myself. It is crucial to always believe in yourself. I am beyond just "believing," because I have arrived. Anytime I hear disparaging remarks through hearsay, I always say that when that person accomplishes half of what I have, I will take them seriously. This industry requires a thick skin at times, but you will find if you're successful at anything, one of the first signs you made it is the naysayers: the ones who say they'll never work with you, knowing they would never have the chance to anyway. It's important to keep rising each time they knock you down, and rise a bit higher each time. "You are like a phoenix...," a mentor once told me and it really is like that.

I am an advocate for the user and consumer on every product I work on. I have held many roles, from artist, to designer, to engineer, all focused on user interface and user experience. In my 10 years in the industry, I have shipped 14+ games on various platforms and developed interfaces for multiple game platforms like Microsoft's Xbox console. I have been a part of two Guinness-World-Record-breaking teams and have taken time to challenge my experience and apply it on products outside of gaming, including Windows Phone OS, Microsoft HoloLens, and various web development projects. Despite everything I have accomplished, I am excited because I know the biggest accomplishments are yet to come. My path has never been secure, but I know taking risks and walking on the edge is the right way for me to go. As Chef Francis Mallmann put it, "… in order to grow and improve you have to be there; a bit at the edge of uncertainty."

No one will open the door for you in this industry, nor will they push you to grow once inside. You have to motivate yourself and push yourself to grow. The door is finally starting to be slightly ajar; it just takes a bit of bravery to step through, especially as a minority.

For everyone who has supported me along the way, I made it.

For my mother, because of the foundation you instilled, I am here.

Endnotes

1. For a good discussion of crunch, read Jason Schreier's "The Horrible World of Video Game Crunch." *Kotaku.* 15 May 2015. Available at http://kotaku.com/crunch-time-why-game-developers-work-such-insane-hours-1704744577
2. Surette, Tim. "EA Settles OT Dispute; Disgruntled 'Spouse' Outed." *Gamespot.* 26 Apr 2006. Available at http://www.gamespot.com/articles/ea-settles-ot-dispute-disgruntled-spouse-outed/1100-6148369/

3. "Developer Satisfaction Survey 2014," IGDA. 25 Jun 2014. Available at https://c.ymcdn.com/sites/www.igda.org/resource/collection/9215B88F-2AA3-4471-B44D-B5D58FF25DC7/IGDA_DSS_2014-Summary_Report.pdf

4. For a particularly heartbreaking explanation of this phenomenon, read Jason Schreier's "Why Game Developers Keep Getting Laid Off." *Kotaku*, 5 Jun 2015. Available at http://kotaku.com/why-game-developers-keep-getting-laid-off-1583192249

8

It Starts in the Classroom
Women and Computer Science

It's not news that computer science programs need more women. Everyone from Sheryl Sandberg to Bill Gates has bemoaned the uneven gender ratios in programming classes. On average, only 18% of students in university computer science programs are women, though colleges like Harvey Mudd have raised that to 40% through active outreach efforts.[1]

Much ink has been spilled over the reasons women might not like programming, from the purely misogynistic (women are too irrational and emotional for such a competitive job[2]), to the discouragement of girls in math and computer classes throughout early education,[3] a tendency of women to prefer personal interaction,[4] and the off-putting effects of joining a program that is already 75% male.[5]

And recent studies show the dearth of female programmers doesn't end at the registrar's office. Of bachelor's degree students enrolling in science, technology, engineering, and mathematics (STEM) majors, 48% will drop out or switch majors before graduating.[6] And even women who stick it out and begin a career in programming often leave later, when continuous sexual microaggressions or lack of support for family life drive female programmers out of company after company.[7]

A Double-Edged Sword

There are advantages and disadvantages to entering the game industry as a coder. Because programmers are in high demand, it can be easier to get that first job. But that same demand makes it hard for companies to turn away male programmers with a history of misogynist or harassing behavior.

Game development is programmer driven. In a given company, programmers make up 35% to 50% of all employees.[8] Almost every game company is in constant need of programmers, with roles like "Server Engineer" and "Gameplay Programmer" in ever-present demand on industry job boards. For a young woman interested in developing games, therefore, learning to code can be a good way to overcome sexist bias—if your company can't launch a game without a server engineer, you're less likely to balk at the kinds of unconscious prejudices that work against women in interviews.

On the other hand, programming in games, as in all tech culture, tends to be the deepest bastion of the "boy's club," and landing a job in programming doesn't mean you'll want to keep that job after years of being torn apart in code reviews while less skilled colleagues are waved through with the penis pass.

Breaking In

If you want to be a game programmer, you'll need either formal training at the university level or extensive experience making games or mods. Important languages and programs to study include

- C and C++. Much AAA game development is done in C++, and nearly all programming jobs require experience in it.
- C# and Javascript. These are the languages required to work in Unity, the most common engine for mobile game development.
- Unreal Engine. UE is now free to use (with payment only on success of the game), and has its own proprietary scripting language.
- Perforce, Sourcetree, Git, SVN, or other version control systems.
- Basic 3D linear algebra, 3D matrix math, and physics are all useful for programming game worlds.

Common Issues

While every company is different, the following problems surface frequently for female programmers. Be prepared to deal with

- *Hostile Code Reviews:* Many programming teams conduct full-team code reviews which pull no punches. Since the culture already rewards joking insults and intimidation, it is easy for those to take a gendered tone when it's a female programmer's work on the line.
- *Credit Stealing:* Many female programmers complain about male colleagues taking credit for their work, either teammates claiming their

accomplishments or critics who ask them to remove work, then rewrite it under their own name.

- *Office Housework:* A single female programmer in a group of men often is expected to do things like refill the coffee pot or take notes at meetings, though these are no more in her job description than those of her male colleagues.
- *Mansplaining:* More than in other disciplines, female programmers tend to face high levels of male colleagues "explaining" things that are a basic part of their job. This can be hostile ("Obviously, you don't understand Java well enough to know why your critique is wrong") or well meaning but condescending ("I can meet with you after the review to explain what I mean").
- *Outright Sexual Harassment:* Programmers, more than other disciplines, tend to attract the stereotypical "geek" persona. And there is an unfortunate tendency in SF/gaming fan communities to brush off outright sexual harassment or stalking as "He has lousy social skills." The blogger Cliff Pervocracy wrote an excellent essay describing the "missing stair" problem that can arise in long-standing social groups (or corporate departments), someone who everyone knows is "kinda creepy," but the old-timers just "step over."[9] When that missing stair is also a talented programmer whom your game relies on, companies can easily turn a blind eye to inappropriate and even illegal behavior.

For Allies

If you're already working in games and looking for ways to make things better, try a few of the following:

- *Blind Resume Reviews:* Studies have shown that blind auditions for musicians lead to 50% more women being hired.[10] Reviewing resumes with the names removed can be a powerful tool for increasing diversity, not just for women but other marginalized groups.
- *Written Code Reviews:* Women are often socialized against face-to-face conflict, so changing your code review format to written critiques may make women more open to both critiquing others and defending their own work.
- *Formal Mentoring:* Many women are eager to find mentors, but be aware of your team: mansplainers, credit stealers, and missing stairs make bad mentors! Mentors should never be allowed to claim credit for

mentees' work, and should always be matched to the mentee's actual (not perceived) level of ability and experience.

Endnotes

1. Miller, Claire Cain. "Some Universities Crack Code in Drawing Women to Computer Science." *New York Times: The Upshot.* 17 Jul 2014. Available at http://www.nytimes.com/2014/07/18/upshot/some-universities-crack-code-in-drawing-women-to-computer-science.html?_r=0&abt=0002&abg=1
2. Vox Day. "You Can Give a Women a CS Degree." Alpha Game Plan (Blog). 27 Feb 2014. Available at http://alphagameplan.blogspot.com/2014/02/you-can-give-woman-cs-degree.html. Contains the gem, "[Female programmers] dropped out because programming demands single-minded focus, mathematical skill, logic, and most of all, individual accountability. They dropped out because they didn't belong in the field and encouraging them to pursue it was doing them a serious career disservice. As a general rule, women don't like competitive jobs where they are held to an objective standard, particularly when they cannot easily pass off their work to others and still take credit for it."
3. Miller, Claire Cain. "How Elementary School Teachers' Biases Can Discourage Girls from Math and Science." *New York Times: The Upshot.* 6 Feb 2015. Available at http://www.nytimes.com/2015/02/07/upshot/how-elementary-school-teachers-biases-can-discourage-girls-from-math-and-science.html?_r=0&abt=0002&abg=1
4. Beltz, Adriene, et al. "Gendered occupational interests: Prenatal androgen effects on psychological orientation to Things versus People." *Hormones and Behavior* Volume 60, Issue 4, September 2011, Pages 313–317.
5. Armstrong, Doree. "More Women Pick Computer Science if Media Nix Outdated 'Nerd' Stereotype." *UW Today,* University of Washington. 25 Jun 2013. Available at http://www.washington.edu/news/2013/06/25/more-women-pick-computer-science-if-media-nix-outdated-nerd-stereotype/
6. US Department of Education. "STEM Attrition: College Students' Paths into and Out of STEM Fields, Statistical Analysis Report." 2013. Page 6. Available at http://nces.ed.gov/pubs2014/2014001rev.pdf
7. Hill, Catherine, et al. "Why So Few: Women in Science, Technology, Engineering and Mathematics." The American Association of University Women. 2010. Page 19. Available at http://www.aauw.org/files/2013/02/Why-So-Few-Women-in-Science-Technology-Engineering-and-Mathematics.pdf
8. Westrar, Johanna, et al. "IGDA Developer Satisfaction Survey 2014, Employment Report." International Game Developers' Association. 2014. Page 13. Available at http://c.ymcdn.com/sites/www.igda.org/resource/collection/9215B88F-2AA3-4471-B44D-B5D58FF25DC7/IGDA_DSS_2014-Employment_Report.pdf
9. Cliff Pervocracy. "The Missing Stair." The Pervocracy (Blog). 22 Jun 2012. Available at http://pervocracy.blogspot.com/2012/06/missing-stair.html
10. Rice, Curt. "How Blind Auditions Helped Orchestras to Eliminate Gender Bias." *The Guardian.* 14 Oct 2013. Available at http://www.theguardian.com/women-in-leadership/2013/oct/14/blind-auditions-orchestras-gender-bias

9

Jane Ng

Environment Artist: *Lord of the Rings: Return of the King*

Senior Artist: *Spore, Brutal Legend, Stacking*

Lead World Artist: *Godfather, The Cave, Firewatch*

I remember eagerly waiting for my dad to come home from his trips to the "computer mall," because he always brought me back something. It was always something fun. One time, he brought me a pet parakeet which knew its name. Sometimes, he brought back computer games, like the Sierra ones with pretty pictures on the boxes. Then one day he came home with a stack of floppy discs bundled in a rubber band and said, "Everyone says this is the hottest new game! Here, have fun." I looked down at the unimpressive pile of discs, saw "Monkey Island" scribbled in pencil, and felt a wave of disappointment. Didn't Dad know I was turning 11 soon? Monkeys are for *little kids*.

To this day, the music for *The Secret of Monkey Island* still transports me back to that moment of wonder and awe when I started up that game for the first time. For a girl accustomed to following rules in the rather traditional confines of an all-girls school in Hong Kong, it was a transformative experience. That game and other subsequent LucasArts adventures showed me a world where creativity reigned, where art has the power to suspend disbelief, and where imagination is the key to all sorts of wonderful puzzles.

One Foot in the Door

Even though video games became less of a defining hobby for me during my teenage years, a sense of longing for that world of creativity and problem solving stayed with me. That thirst eventually led me to Swarthmore College, a liberal arts college near Philadelphia, PA, where I could explore my inter-disciplinary interests in art and engineering. While I enjoyed my engineering courses, in particular the computer graphics classes, I came to realize I was much more interested in "using the tools" to make beautiful images than "creating the tools" as an engineer. As I was considering changing my major to fine arts (but retaining a minor in engineering), I came across a copy of *Cinefex*, a quarterly journal for visual effects in movies.

Flipping through the little book of wonders, the name LucasFilm leapt out at me. LucasFilm, like LucasFilm Games? Were they related to LucasArts, the source of so much of my childhood joy? I did not know how the com-panies were linked, but *Cinefex* was a showcase of the kind of imaginative creativity that I wanted so much to be a part of. Visual effects seemed to be the field where people like me, who were passionate about inventive problem solving and beautiful images, ended up. I instantly wanted to know more.

Without any connections in the industry, I started randomly e-mailing dif-ferent visual effects people to ask for advice. I chanced upon Terrence Masson, who was working at Industrial Light & Magic (ILM), the effects division of LucasFilm, at the time, and he became a mentor to me. He was generous with his time, and a path to visual effects as a career was becoming clear. Just as I was looking for a summer internship, however, he decided to leave ILM and join the game industry. The game industry? You mean there are people whose job it is to make video games? Before that point, I never realized game develop-ment was actually a job one could have. With a little hesitation, I followed my mentor into games and ended up spending the summer of my junior year at a small game company called Ronin Entertainment in Novato, CA.

It was a great summer. I felt a unique kinship with the game developers I met there, because not only had they all heard of the games I grew up with, the founders of Ronin came from LucasArts and some had worked on those games that meant so much to me. As an immigrant who was used to being a cultural outsider to most American trivia, being with people who could share jokes about Guybrush Threepwood felt a bit like finding my tribe. Forget visual effects, games were where I could make my home.

You're Hired

I moved to California after graduation despite not having a committed job offer from Ronin. I naively thought if I made myself indispensable to the company on the cheap they would have to hire me full time. This is definitely not something I would recommend to any student now, but I was tremendously fortunate that my audacious gamble actually turned into something like an apprenticeship. I spent the next two years learning the basics of video game art production from my wonderfully gracious co-workers.

By 2003, as Ronin's prospects declined, many of my co-workers left for Electronic Arts to work on *Lord of the Rings: Return of the King*. Upon their recommendation, I also joined the team as a temporary full-time (TFT) environment artist. There were many TFTs on the project and rumor was that only one permanent full-time position would be available at the end. I don't recall feeling competitive; I only remember how excited I was to be at a *real* studio. This was exactly the kind of project I had always dreamed of being a part of, even before I had the vocabulary to express it.

For five months, I tried to learn everything I could. I sought out more work when what was on my plate was done, not out of a sense of corporate duty or a desire to impress management (I barely knew what management was!) but out of sheer enthusiasm to contribute as much as I could to the game. I loved *Lord of the Rings*, and here I was, given a chance to put my mark on a small bit of its universe. I was in heaven.

There was one specific incident that may have won me the full-time position. Near the end of production, Glen Schofield (the art executive producer) gathered the art team and asked if anyone would take the initiative to make level maps for the strategy guide. I volunteered, thinking it was a fun problem to solve amid the mundanity of bug fixing. Later that day, when Glen walked by my cubicle I signaled for him to come check out my work-in-progress. He took one quick look, nodded, and said "These look great. You're hired," and continued on his way. At first, I thought it was just an offhand remark like "good job," but a week later I found out I was indeed the only TFT to receive a permanent, full-time position.

During this early phase of my career, I was not consciously aware how few women were in games, because there were women working close to me in authoritative positions. I looked up to Arcadia Kim, who was a senior producer and very prominent in all team communications. There were three other women in the environment art team of about 15. Granted, if you consider the number of women across the whole team, the percentage was still rather low, but on a daily basis I never felt out of place.

Godfather

About a year later, during the development of *Godfather*, I was promoted to be one of the youngest lead environment artists at EA. I was overjoyed and was ready to prove my mettle on this difficult open-world project. Around the same time I started hearing whispers from some women co-workers about how "It doesn't matter if you did well, you have to keep proving yourself over and over again." At first, I was puzzled … given my promotion, surely they were wrong? Were they bitter that they didn't get a chance to be lead? I shrugged off the sentiment at first, but as I started encountering resistance while doing what I thought was responsible work as a lead, I started to wonder if the other women there were onto something.

It was never anything conspicuous. No incident on its own would conclusively point to any bias. If I spoke up about any individual instance, it would sound petty, even to my own ears. Nobody ever called attention to my gender (though I did intentionally start dressing older, because I felt self-conscious about being merely 25), but I started to notice that many of my well-reasoned suggestions to a newly hired art director were taken quite negatively.

Informing an art director (especially one with no prior game production experience) about the methodology of asset creation was part of my job as a lead artist. It was also my responsibility to provide my team of more than 10 environment modelers with realistic goals that they could meet with our asset pipeline. Setting my team up for success sometimes meant telling the art director that his pursuit of filmic photorealism was constrained not by me, nor the team's talent, but by the limitations of the PlayStation 2.

During my performance reviews, I was often rated as Over Target in many aspects of work, and consistently given salary raises alongside the praise. However, as production went forward, various managers started to interact with me in a manner that suggested they thought I had a problem that was unrelated to my work performance. They started by saying I should work on my teamwork skills (while peers continued to tell me I was a joy to work with). Then came suggestions that I had an "attitude problem" (without any clarification on what that meant). Finally one day over an intra-office phone call I was informed by a sympathetic development director that apparently the art director had complained directly to human resources about how I was being "insubordinate," but that I should not worry because the art director was not actually my boss.

I was shocked. I remember feeling so shaken that I couldn't say much in response during the phone call, though a voice inside my mind screamed, "If I were a 34-year-old man this would not be happening to me." How was subordination in any way expected of any other lead? All the cumulative slights and microaggressions that I could individually shrug off came tumbling into focus at that moment.

The rest of *Godfather*'s development was tough for me. The high of being a lead artist was being chipped away by various "incidents," and was displaced by a building sense of disillusionment.

In the latter half of development, a new senior artist joined the team and started questioning the art creation process the team had settled on. Through various political channels, he suggested a radically different approach to world building and

Microaggressions

If you spend any time reading about feminist issues in business, you'll come across the term "microaggressions,"[1] which was first coined by Columbia professor Derald Wing Sue to describe "brief and commonplace daily verbal, behavioral, or environmental indignities, whether intentional or unintentional, that communicate hostile, derogatory, or negative racial slights and insults."[2] This idea has come to refer to all of the small, often unconscious ways in which people reinforce stereotypes in ways that are damaging to women and minorities.

For women in gaming and the broader tech culture, this can encompass everything from female testers automatically getting assigned to test cooking and babysitting games, to company founders being assumed to be their co-founder's secretary, to having to work in an office filled with pin-up art. Women can even frequently face microaggressions from other women, who might ridicule a more feminine-behaving woman as not being "one of the boys."[3]

What's "aggressive" about these behaviors isn't necessarily ill intent on the part of the men and women doing them. It's that to the person on the receiving end, no matter how easily overlooked each of those little slights is individually, they add up to the unmistakable message that "you don't belong here." If you are always mistaken for one of your employees' non-game-dev wife, if you are constantly told that "girls don't like" the games you play, if people stop talking when you come into the room and you know it's because they don't want "Mom" to hear their dirty jokes, it becomes hard not to wonder whether you picked the wrong line of work. The reaction to Ellen Pao's failed discrimination suit against Kleiner Perkins showed how familiar most women in tech are with the cumulative effect of all of this not-directly-harassing behavior, while most men remain happily oblivious.[4]

Editor

promised that with his new method the team could deliver better and more assets given the same schedule. I disagreed based on my experience. I had worked directly with the team since Day One of preproduction, and knew that with no tool improvements planned, unproven processes were risky at best. Data proved to me that while our approach left much to be desired, it was realistically the best way to meet our challenging production requirements on a tight deadline. To my dismay, management decided to place their bets on this new artist who promised the moon, and removed me as the art lead.

Not three months later, after the new guy unsurprisingly missed all of his promised delivery, I was unceremoniously reinstated as a lead artist. My manager confided to me that he knew they had made a mistake in not trusting my judgment, at the cost of precious development time that we couldn't spare. Before the end of the project, the art director whose view of hierarchy I had so challenged was quietly removed from power and then laid off. So was the new guy with the extravagant plan. I shipped the game as a lead artist and was again promoted and given a substantial raise.

Invisible Club

But by then, it wasn't about being proven right, or who got their comeuppance. While the powers that be ultimately rewarded me, I was a very different developer at the end of the project. I recalled the grumblings of my fellow women co-workers in the past, and could suddenly see through their lens to recognize a level of implicit trust among people who belonged in an invisible "club" that I was not a member of. If you were one of the "bros," you would be trusted over a minority woman top performer even if you were new to the team or had no prior experience at all.

It's important to note that to this day I never thought any of those co-workers were sexists. I don't think any of them believed I was less than my male colleagues because I am a woman. The issue was that a group of well-meaning professionals could still perpetuate a sexist culture where women were continuously put through trials to prove their worth, over and over on issues large and small, at their expense. Unconscious bias is a long-term psychological and emotional tax that creates a very draining environment in which passion can be ground to dust. Arcadia Kim, the producer I looked up to, rose to become chief operating officer (COO) of EA Los Angeles and then left the industry after a couple of years. Out of the four female environment artists on my *Lord of the Rings* team, I am the only one still in the industry.

Conclusion

So, after all that, what kept me around? I decided I would actively seek out a different work environment that made a better life for myself. At the end of *Godfather*, I requested a transfer to *Spore* under the guidance of Lucy Bradshaw, who had often publicly stressed the importance of having a diverse development team. Later, after four years at Electronic Arts, I left to join Double Fine Productions. There I would have some of my most fulfilling work experiences with Tim Schafer and Ron Gilbert, whose work on *The Secret of Monkey Island* had inspired me to become a game artist in the first place. Currently, I am at Campo Santo, where we just shipped our first game, *Firewatch*.

Screenshot from Firewatch, *Campo Santo, 2016*

The absolute joy of creating game art still outshines the dark times for me. It is magical to be able to create worlds where others can lose themselves. The sense of camaraderie and pride one builds with a development team is also tremendously rewarding. I wouldn't want to live without any of those things, despite all the extra hurdles that are in my path because I am categorically different than 90% of my colleagues. To me, games are still the celebration of creativity and imagination that I once dreamed they would be.

Endnotes

1. For an excellent discussion of microaggressions in tech, read Livio de la Cruz's article, "Stop Acting So Surprised: How Microaggressions Enforce Stereotypes in Tech." *Model View Culture*. 30 Jun 2015. Available at https://modelviewculture.com/pieces/stop-acting-so-surprised-how-microaggressions-enforce-stereotypes-in-tech

2. Sue, Derald Wing, et al. "Racial Microaggressions in Everyday Life." *American Psychologist*, Volume 62, Issue 4, May–Jun 2007. Pages 271–286.

3. For an excellent discussion of how internalized sexism turns female gamers against each other, read The Border House blog, "Diamonds in the Rough and Those Other Girls: Conflicts between Female Gamers." http://borderhouseblog.com/?p=791

4. Gannes, Liz. "The Real Precedent in the Ellen Pao Case Happened Out of Court." Re/Code. 28 Mar 2015. Available at http://recode.net/2015/03/28/the-real-precedent-in-the-ellen-pao-case-happened-out-of-court/

10

Kimberly Unger

Designer: *Agiliste, PuzzlingUs, SmashTastic*

Author: *Game Development Essentials: Mobile Game Development, The Official Game Salad Guide to Game Design*

Chief Executive Officer/Founder: Bushi-go, Inc.

Humans like straight lines. When you're in high school, trying to figure out what you want to be if you grow up, it seems like a simple thing. You choose what you want to be, and you pursue that goal with single-minded determination. In the stories you hear, the successes you read about, the biographies of the heroes you look up to, it seems like that's exactly what they did. They decided who they were going to be and they fought their way there. One line, end to end.

I didn't get here by following a straight line. Sometimes, I think it would be nice if I had, that I would be taken *much more seriously* if I had, but more often I feel that the cross-chatter between my related disciplines is much too valuable to just wish away. My take on games and the things that drive them is fairly unique, and I don't think I'd trade that for anything.

The Backstory

I created my first game in 1983 when BASIC was still a viable programming language and COBOL ruled the business world. I was proud of it then, and I'm still proud of it now. It was an "endless shooter" game based around the world of Anne McCaffrey's *Dragonquest*. You flew your little 8-bit dragon around blasting things out of the sky with fire until you died three times. Clean, simple, and perfectly in line with what "consoles" and arcades were dishing out at the time.

The end result was entered in a local competition and won first prize for the game category. That event was the first time I ever encountered the idea that I might not be welcome in computing. The rest of the mostly male class let me know the award was entirely undeserved. I had asked another student in the class for help with the programming elements that were beyond my skill and any of my contributions to the game were therefore irrelevant. This was not an unusual situation. There was a group of students in my school who were happy to inform me that I didn't belong in any activity I chose, particularly ones I excelled at, so this kind of thing was par for the course.

I went to the student who had helped me and offered him the award. I had credited his work in the game. I had done everything I could think of to make it clear that the product was not mine alone. I didn't know what else to do and keeping a friend was far more important. To his absolute credit, he told me they were wrong and should all get stuffed (paraphrasing here). As a side note, that student went on to become a lead engineer in this industry and still remains on my list of "best friends who will help me hide a body."

But I didn't want to spend any more of my free time in the computer lab after that.

Girls and Computers

When I started working with computers in middle school, the issue was never "girls don't like technology" or "girls can't code." Instead, it was the rather banal case of "tween girls shouldn't be hanging out in darkened rooms full of tween boys." My perception was always that there was something "wrong" with being the only girl in the room, though no adult ever said why.

As much as I loved computers and games, it became clear they were yet another thing I would have to fight to stay involved with, against other students and eventually against teachers (especially at the college level) and family members (who have been supportive, but still encourage me to quit every couple of years). At 12 years old, I was looking for a place where I didn't have to argue every single time just to be allowed to play.

Games, however, would prove to be a lure stronger than a handful of grumpy tween boys.

I went to University of California, Davis, for an English degree. And after a hiatus of about six years, I got back into computing. Not through the regular channels, mind you. I attempted to take an introductory programming course, but was told by the teacher to reconsider because (a) I had no "real" programming experience (BASIC and TurboPascal were no longer even on the radar); (b) I was the only girl and would therefore be miserable; and (c) there was a waitlist of students who needed the course for their degree, and I was taking it as an elective, so shame on me.

Instead, I reentered programming through a new group of friends, whom I had begun playing *Dungeons and Dragons* with during my sophomore year. Some were CS students and some were simply computer-enthusiasts. They helped me set up my first e-mail account and get onto things like Usenet and the alt.net forums on the SUN stations in the basement computer labs. I learned how to work with a UNIX command line. I also learned to never, ever identify as female online: no female names, nothing about your gender in your finger file, *no, not ever are you nuts*!? I got to play MUDs and MUCKs and watched a friend flush his degree down the toilet trying to run and maintain his own BBS. I learned how to edit hex files and that there was a soda machine at University of California, Santa Cruz (a hundred miles away), that you could ping to find out how many sodas it had left and what flavors they were.

It was all learning by osmosis, by experimentation, by getting in and breaking things to see how they were put together, or, more importantly, watching other people break things so I could learn what I needed without having to put up yet another fight. There were no formal classes I could access, and I'm not entirely sure I would have learned what I needed there, so I became an expert in do-it-yourself learning.

It was also, at that time, perfectly useless at the end of the day. I had no programming experience, and had no way to get any, and so I would have to find another way to get into making games.

DOOM and the Rise of the MOD Communities

When I got out of school, I went to work as a registered assistant in the financial services industry, eventually getting my broker's license (which meant I could trade, but not have my own client list). In the evenings, after the markets closed, I would get together with a group of friends and we would play *DOOM*, a shareware product that was currently the hottest freaking thing on the market. It was awesome. One person would play and the rest would watch and we would swap in and out (because only one of us actually had a computer that would run it).

But then they opened the game to modding. You could stick your co-worker's heads onto the imps and blast away; you could build entirely new levels. It gave me exactly what I needed. A way to tear apart a game so that I could learn. With *DOOM* and its successors, I learned about Object-Oriented programming. I was able to take the code for an in-game enemy, tear it apart to figure out what made it tick, then put it back together to suit the kind of enemy I wanted it to be. I was again able to teach myself everything I wanted to know without having to explain *why* I wanted to know all these things.

Art School

I went back to school again, this time to get a degree that would directly position me for working in games and entertainment. I had a focus now. I had a portfolio of work that was made up of almost entirely self-taught art and computer animation. I had applied for jobs in local studios more than once (even Westwood Studios gave me an interview) but my skills were too unfocused, too random. I didn't fit a role. I had a great understanding of how computing systems worked and how to fix them, I was a passable graphic artist, I had experience in business and finance, but not enough of any one thing to make me a fit.

So, I took my self-taught computer knowledge, my rendered-at-home 3D animations, and entered the Illustration major at the Art Center College of Design (ACCD). (There were no majors available anywhere in games or computer entertainment at the time.) From there I consulted with the dean of my department and managed to craft a degree that was not purely Illustration, but rather some bastard hybrid of Illustration/Production/Trans and 3D.

Make Them Say No

I have adopted a policy of "Make them say no," in large part because of my experiences at ACCD. Even among artists, my expertise in technology made me an outlier, so in order to get the classes I wanted (which were often part of the Trans and Production majors), I had to be confident. The question was always "How far can I push without pissing off my Dean." The answer is always, "When they say no, take it with grace. *Until* they say no, you stay on it like a rat on a French fry."

Before the end of my sophomore year, I was working as a lab assistant to help pay for my classes, and by the end of my junior year I had been invited to teach 3D modeling and animation for the brand new Maya. I got my first industry gig as the only artist working for a video-game startup backed by Donald Trump, and I paid for my last year of school by developing course materials for and teaching Alias and Maya at the Art Center College of Design and the University of Santa Monica.

Industry Bound

By the end of my senior year, I had run the gamut of interviews with the major game studios in Los Angeles. ACCD's career center didn't yet have a line into the game industry, so I started with entertainment studios, pulling short-term gigs on TV commercials and feature films. For games I was on my own. The questions asked from the big studios were things like "Do you *play* any games?" (At the time, shooters like *DOOM II*, and adventure games like *Tomb Raider* were my bailiwick.) Or "It's unusual for a woman to work in games, what made you decide on this career path?" Or the ever present, "You'll be the only woman on a team of all men, are you *sure* you're okay with that?" Needless to say, none of those interviewers ever called me back.

Ironically, it was almost always the nongamers who were surprised that a woman would make games. These were often people who came into the game industry through other routes, from Business or Human Resources or Marketing. The experienced industry professionals I worked with, whether they be programmers or designers or artists, rarely batted an eye.

Other Job Paths

This book only had room to focus on a finite number of occupations within the game industry. However, the careers included are far from the only ways to work with video games. Other industry jobs include

- *Marketing:* A game's marketing is just as important to its success as its quality. Large game companies and publishers usually have extensive marketing departments made up of people with backgrounds in marketing comics or film or other media.
- *Editing:* Not every game company employs writers on staff, and even fewer keep dedicated editors, but this number is slowly increasing. Editing jobs at game companies can range from contract copyeditors to on-staff editors who can rewrite dialogue, prep VO scripts and serve as the keepers of IP continuity across multiple game franchises.[1]
- *Audio:* Game audio is an important specialty, including everything from the game's score (requiring composers and musicians), to sound effects, to voiced dialogue (requiring VO directors and voice actors, in addition to the audio engineers who put that dialogue in-game) and even interfacing with player voice commands, if working with systems like the Kinect.
- *Localization:* Game translation and localization departments need multilingual, organized, great communicators to work with actors and audio departments in other countries, while making sure writers and designers make clear the intent of every line and idiom in their game.
- *Finance:* Large game companies need the same kinds of financial

Eventually, I found a position with another game startup, this time working on the PlayStation 1 version of *You Don't Know Jack*. From there, I was recruited by a headhunter to work as an artist in San Francisco on *Tetris Worlds*, again for a small studio. I began to attend Game Developers Conference (GDC) and made a concerted effort to meet more people in my industry. Instead of becoming a stay-at-home mom with the birth of my first child (born the same day the *Tetris Worlds* build went Gold), I became a freelancer.

Hanging Out My Shingle

Being a freelancer, especially as a games generalist with a reputation for being able to "fix anything," turned out to be the best exposure I ever got. I worked as a troubleshooter/triage specialist for a number of big studios, filling in for lead artists/art director positions until full-time employees could be found, working on a range of titles from AAA sports titles to mobile games. Most of the time, I would be hired by the producer on an as-needed or short-term basis. Many of these turned into formal job offers, but because I had small children at home and wanted the total flexibility I had as a freelancer, I turned them down.

I began to pitch my own games to studios and develop working relationships with programmers and other artists in the industry. We have a crazy turnover rate. Despite what companies will tell you about benefits and 401k's, there's a good chance you will be let go at the end of any given project. I saved money from my freelancing and hired people I knew as contractors between bouts of employment. Sometimes, I'd get them for a week, sometimes a month, but it allowed me to put together demos for my original game designs. I had to develop a modular system for designing, because I never knew who would be able to work on what for how long. I learned to manage all different kinds of personalities. I improved my own programming skills (again, all DIY coding) to fill the gaps. Coupled with my art-training and literary background, my ability to build functional demos improved and started to pick up actual publication interest.

officers and payroll specialists as in any other large company.

- *Human Resources/Recruitment:* Game company HR departments require HR specialists who love games enough that they can pick out a passionate job candidate and explain the ins-and-outs of a development job to new employees.

- *Other Support Roles:* Large game companies often employ receptionists, assistants, and other support staff. While not as glamorous as a developer position, these roles can give you the opportunity to get swag and play games and learn about development without being subject to the same long hours and high turnover as development jobs.

Editor

Screenshot from Veiled Alliances, *Bushi-Go, 2015*

Networking

Every meeting, chance or otherwise, is networking. Making all of those connections over the years means I have shaken hands with many industry professionals at many stages of our respective careers. Everyone evolves over time—you learn new things, get new jobs, start companies, get married, crash and burn—so even if you don't have common ground now, there's a good chance you will later on.

Eventually, I started a formal company with the help of an assistant producer I had met at ACCD. We had attempted to pitch episodic-content games to the major studios when Xbox Live was first announced, and with the rise of smartphone gaming, we decided to take another run at it, this time as an independent development house for mobile, rather than AAA games.

Denouement

I am still flogging my company, Bushi-Go, into existence. Tech news outlets tell you this is easy: get a group of five friends, set up in someone's garage, build a game for funzies and WHAMMO, you have a hit. (I think most of the women in this book can tell you otherwise!) When I teach classes in Game Art and Design, I see this idea in new students all the time. But when you talk honestly to anyone out there who has "made it" you'll hear similar stories. There are always multiple points of failure, or at least a lot of "average" along the way. Teams split and re-form, ideas get scooped, employees and contractors get hired away. Just as the path into the industry can be crooked, so can the path *within* the industry; the line never straightens.

But that means it's your determination that will define you; that's what keeps you on that path. We humans might like straight lines, but we don't *need* them if we follow our passion.

Endnote

1. Cameron Harris gave a talk about game editing at GDC 2014, now available on the GDC vault at: http://gdcvault.com/play/1020029/You-Need-an-Editor

11

"You Must Be an Artist"
Stereotypes and Realities about Female Game Artists

For some reason, many people assume that if a woman is a "real" game developer (not a "soft" job like production), she must be an artist. Perhaps this is because "artistic" fits well into feminine stereotypes. Whatever the reason, this perception is not matched by reality, in which a full 91% of game artists and animators are male, making it second only to programming as the most male-dominated profession. By comparison, 22% of producers and 13% of designers are female.[1] Outside the game industry, the numbers are dead even, with women making up 51% of currently working visual artists and earning half of all master of fine arts (MFA) degrees.[2]

So, why the disparity in gaming? To start with, female game artists and animators make $21,000 less per year than their male counterparts on average,[3] and gender-biased hiring practices quickly become a self-fulfilling prophecy as people (read, "men") with greater experience get promoted to art director roles and hire more people like themselves. In 2012, when the #1reasonwhy hashtag exploded on Twitter to answer why more women don't become game creators, female game artists shared such woes as "#1reasonwhy Once heard an Art manager say 'We don't need any more women, they're more trouble than they're worth' as he viewed applications" and "Because I got blank stares when I asked why a female soldier in a game I worked on looked like a porn star. #1reasonwhy."

But art is arguably exactly where games need more female input. The visual look is the first part of a game that players encounter, on the box jacket or in ads, before they even sit down to play. When that art has two goals—to cater to male power fantasies with an endless parade of buff bald guys, and to cater to male sexual fantasies with half-naked women—it sends a clear message to female players.

For years, players have complained about oversexed female characters who exist only to titillate male players. (Google turns up 126,000 results on the search "oversexed video game characters.") Even franchises with popular, tough female protagonists, like Samus Aran in the *Metroid* series, compromise their own character by revealing her in either a one-piece bathing suit or a bikini at the end, depending on how quickly you beat the game.[4]

And game art departments are notorious for sticking their feet in their mouths any time someone mentions their female characters might be problematic. In 2013, when Blizzard's game director was interviewed about *Heroes of the Storm*, he was asked whether the female characters would be hypersexualized. His response ran the gamut from dismissive to uncomfortable, first claiming that the game wanted a "comic book sensibility," and then saying defensively, "We're not running for president. We're not sending a message."[5] And in 2014, developer Ubisoft was widely mocked for saying that they literally couldn't afford to animate a female character, "because it's double the animations, double the voices and all that stuff, and double the visual assets."[6]

When your art department is 91% men, it can seem universally funny to show your powerful female character in a bikini as a "reward," or like a waste of time to create a playable female protagonist. It may even start to seem like all lady characters must have gigantic breasts that need their own physics[7] and a special hip-swaying walk that makes it impossible to share animations with male characters. But add a few women to that room, and it's a lot more likely that those choices will be questioned before the inevitable Internet backlash.

For Allies

If you're already a game artist or animator, there are some things you can do to support women in your field.

- *Question Visual Design Choices:* Don't leave it up to the one woman in the room to say if a character design is oversexualized. Mention it yourself if male characters are in full body armor and female characters are running around in bikinis.

- *Include a Greater Representation of Body Types:* Many games are criticized for having a wide range of male characters (including old men, fat men, buff leading-man types, and comic relief), while all female characters conform to a single, young, thin, conventionally attractive form.
- *Include More Eye-Candy for the Ladies:* At GDC 2014, Michelle Clough brought the house down with her talk, "Fewer Tifas or More Sephiroths: Male Sexualization in Video Games,[8]" in which she spoke frankly about her crushes on attractive game characters. If your art department gets squicky and homophobic about discussing male characters' "hotness," remind them that not only are half their potential players female, a tenth of them are gay, and they will all appreciate having their attraction respected.

You may notice that these suggestions are about the art in your games, not the behavior in your departments. That's because those go together. A male artist who can talk frankly about the attractiveness of the dude he's drawing is also an artist who won't get defensive when someone tells him his lady warrior needs better armor, and a man who won't be intimidated to work for a female boss. And a game with realistic and diverse female body types is a game that more women will play and that will inspire women to create their own fan art and cosplays and eventually realize that they can become game artists themselves.

Becoming a Game Artist or Animator

Game art is an immense field with far more specialties than can fit here. Game artists can create hand-drawn 2D concept art, render or rig 3D models in Maya or 3ds Max, design textures, animate fight scenes, create tiny facial animations to bring genuine emotion to conversations and hundreds of other things. If you're interested in becoming a game artist, it is helpful to

- Have a thorough understanding of the history of animation in film, anime, and videogames.
- Be conversant with programs such as Adobe Photoshop, Adobe Illustrator, Maya, and/or 3ds Max.
- Have a strong background as a visual artist. Even if you work mainly on the computer, you want a strong understanding of basic illustration … for purposes of quickly scribbling an example on a whiteboard during meetings, if nothing else.
- Get a degree or complete a certificate program in an art- or animation-related field.
- Maintain an up-to-date portfolio of your work that is easily accessible online.

Endnotes

1. "Gamasutra's Annual Game Developer's Salary Survey." 2015. Pages 2–3. Available at http://www.gamesetwatch.com/2014/09/05/GAMA14_ACG_SalarySurvey_F.pdf

2. National Museum of Women in the Arts. "Get the Facts." Available at http://nmwa.org/advocate/get-facts

3. "Gamasutra's Annual Game Developer's Salary Survey." 2015. Page 2. Available at http://www.gamesetwatch.com/2014/09/05/GAMA14_ACG_SalarySurvey_F.pdf

4. Desta, Yohana. "The Shocking Evolution of Eight Iconic Female Gaming Characters." 30 Sep 2014. Available at http://mashable.com/2014/09/30/female-game-characters/

5. Grayson, Nathan. "Blizzard on Heroes of the Storm, Female Designs in MOBAs." 22 Nov 2013. Available at http://www.rockpapershotgun.com/2013/11/22/blizzard-on-heroes-of-the-storm-female-designs-in-mobas/

6. Farokhmanesh, Megan. "Ubisoft Abandoned Women Assassins in Co-op Because of the Additional Work." 10 Jun 2014. Available at http://www.polygon.com/e3-2014/2014/6/10/5798592/assassins-creed-unity-female-assassins%20

7. Hernandez, Patricia. "How Video Game Breasts Are Made (And How They Can Go Wrong)." Kotaku. 24 Feb 2015. Available at http://kotaku.com/how-video-game-breasts-are-made-and-why-they-can-go-so-1687753475

8. Clough, Michelle. "Fewer Tifas or More Sephiroths: Male Sexualization in Video Games." The Game Developer's Conference. 2014. Available on the GDC Vault at http://www.gdcvault.com/play/1020520/Fewer-Tifas-or-More-Sephiroths

12

Laralyn McWilliams

Games: *Shadows, Crags, Stitch: Experiment 626, Full Spectrum Warrior, Fear & Respect, Free Realms, James Patterson: Catch a Killer, Relic Quest, PWND*

I discovered in 1982 that my purpose in life is to make video games.

It was 12 years between the time I first said I wanted to make video games for a living, and when I actually started doing it. That would be fine if I first realized I wanted to make games when I was six … but I was 16. I think much of the delay was due to the expectations at the time for what women did and didn't do.

Making Worlds

My first inkling of what would become the main element of my life was when I was eight years old. My father was stationed at what was then Oakland Army Base, and one summer we drove down to Los Angeles to go to Disneyland. If you'd asked me on the drive down what I wanted to be when I grew up, I would have said, "A writer."

After I went on *Pirates of the Caribbean* and *The Haunted Mansion*, I said, "They're making worlds! I want to make worlds." This was 1973. This was before I'd even seen *Pong*. My family was an early adopter of video games, and we did eventually have *Pong*, then later an Atari. I played those games a lot, but didn't connect the arcade experiences with "making worlds."

Fast forward to the early 1980s, at the end of my junior year of high school. I got interested in a couple of guys who hung out in the computer lab. So I hung out in the computer lab, where there were three Apple II's. It didn't take long for me to realize the Apple II's were more interesting than the guys, so I started trying to figure them out.

I went to a very large high school, and I'm sure there was at least one computer class. Even though I was in AP science and math, the possibility of taking programming was never mentioned to me by any teacher or counselor. Still, I was fascinated by the Apple II's. I taught myself to use them, and then I started teaching myself BASIC.

My fascination grew until I talked my parents into getting me a home computer: a TI-99/4A. The TI-99/4A was a hybrid console/computer that hooked up to your TV. You could insert cartridges of various arcade games, and you could code in BASIC, but there was no built-in storage. When you turned the machine off, your code was gone.

I played arcade games on it, but I really wanted to program. I spent months laboriously typing in programs from magazines to see what they did, and learning how to make my own programs. Every night I would type in code; every day I'd shut the machine off and the code would be gone. Eventually, I discovered you could save your code if you had a tape recorder and a special cable. I had a tape recorder, and I'd just learned to drive.

I borrowed Mom's car, went down to the computer store (Babbages) and discovered not just the required cable but a whole section with new kinds of games. I only had enough money for one, so I chose carefully and went home with my new cable and Scott Adams' *Adventure*.

Playing *Adventure* was the moment it came together for me. People were creating worlds on computers—interactive ones! That was what I wanted to do. That weekend I made my first text adventure. It was about being on a deserted island with a cute guy. What can I say? I was 16.

Still No Formal Training

I continued coding weird little games on my home computer throughout my senior year. I still never took computer classes at school, even when I went to college the next year. I genuinely never considered studying programming, even though my campus job was being an operator on the giant VAX computer in the basement. I suspect I was the only female VAX operator, although it never occurred to me to ask ... or even notice.

I eventually got a Mac 512ke and a printer. That's when I stopped going to parties and started going into as many game worlds as I could. I spent half my time playing and half my time trying to code. With two years of college left, games became my primary focus, yet it still never occurred to me to take a single programming class. It wasn't until years later that I would wonder why. A great segment on NPR called *When Women Stopped Coding*[1] provides a summary of how societal perceptions of technology and computers changed in the 1970s, how it became a hobby "for men," and how the presence of women in technology started to decline.

So I graduated from college, worked as a secretary for a while and thought about how to make a living long term. Meanwhile, I was fixing all the computers in the office, and coding or playing games all night and weekend. I eventually worked as a legal secretary and decided maybe I could make a career in law, so I went to law school.

Three years later, I had a law degree but the call of technology was even stronger—so strong that I declined offers to join Legal Aid and instead worked as a tech writer at a software company in North Carolina, SEER Technologies. The software was quite complex (a large-scale CASE tool for client-server data management) and I suggested interactive training. We also gave big client shows, so I steered the company toward multimedia. I was finally starting to create interactive works, even if they weren't games.

Finding *Myst*

Then everything changed: I played *Myst*. It was the first time I'd seen a game approach the fidelity and immersion of Disney attractions. The developers made a vibrant world with (at the time) photorealistic images and you-are-there audio. I was stunned. Then I was depressed; why wasn't *I* doing this? And then I became motivated.

I started working nights and weekends on my Mac LC. I taught myself better scripting in Director and 3D graphics with Strata, the software they used to create art in *Myst*. Eventually, I had a demo to show to a local game company, Random Games. Together, we sold the demo to Microprose. I was off! Finally, in 1994, 12 years after I first knew I wanted to make games for a living, I was actually doing it.

Over the years, my job title has changed. At first, there were no titles; everyone on the small teams just worked together. When I first joined a larger company, "design" didn't exist as a discipline, so I was a producer. Eventually, the industry matured and I had to make a choice. It wasn't much of a debate for me: I was a game designer. I always had been.

For the first 15 years of my career, when anyone asked me what it was like to be a woman in game development, I had a standard answer. A joke: "Well, there's never a line for the women's bathroom at GDC!" Then I'd laugh and change the subject. In 2001, women made up only 6% of game developers[2]—and that was higher than the mid-1990s. Back then, none of us really talked about being a woman; I wanted my gender to be irrelevant, so I made sure it was.

That doesn't mean I didn't encounter sexism. It ranged from casual exclusion from company lunches, events, and even meetings (especially when those meetings were held in strip clubs!) all the way to open statements like "I hope this goes better than the last time we had a woman in the producer's meeting." Things like that felt minor to me, compared to my passion for games. I considered it part of the cost, like the need to relocate or work long hours to ship a milestone.

I worked on a bunch of really different games over the years, ranging from kid's games like *Stitch: Experiment 626* (PS2 shooter/platformer) and *Free Realms* (PC/PS3 MMO) to one of the most hardcore military strategy games ever on console (*Full Spectrum Warrior*, Xbox). You can call it eclectic or schizophrenic, depending on your point of view. Unlike many of my colleagues who were quick to say they only wanted to work on "games they would play," I just wanted to make great games for any audience.

A side effect of that eclectic career is that I saw firsthand the difference in how people and teams are treated when they make games for kids or women versus "core" games (still largely made for men). It infuriated me. Teams for kids' and women's games were almost always handed a film or TV license, understaffed, given a year or less, and generally treated like second-class citizens.

Taking Stock

I started to see the climate change around women in game development around the year 2010. Women started speaking about their experiences, some quietly and some loudly. I became an outspoken advocate for changing our attitude about what I called "alternative audiences" (like kids and women) … but not about my experiences as a woman actually working in game development. On that, I stayed silent.

Then, in March 2012, I was diagnosed with Stage IV tonsil cancer. I worked from home as I went through chemo and radiation, which meant I had a lot of time to think about my life and the choices I had made. I thought about what really mattered to me. I thought about my purpose: Why was I here?

I started to speak, very quietly, very pragmatically, about the experiences of women in game development. I focused on my actual experiences. I wrote about the need to be objective when women share difficult experiences with us. I finally said yes to a few interviews about "women in games."

The backlash was clear and immediate. Those discussions were met with open hostility from some colleagues. At one point, I was told directly that any discussion of women's experiences in game development was like debating religion and politics—it wasn't just divisive, it was "off topic" in a game development group. I said in response that I thought of myself as a game developer first and a woman second. When those words left my mouth, I was stunned. Not just because I'd said them, but because in that moment, I meant them. I felt gutted by the clear exclusion of my colleagues and awareness of my own complicity.

It's still hard for me to talk about that moment, because the rejection came from people who were my peers—my friends—for 10, 15, sometimes 20 years. It made me think about how much I had unconsciously decided what parts of myself I was willing to show. I hadn't talked about being a woman, or about so many things. Over time, not showing or discussing those aspects of myself eroded them until they ceased to exist. I had actually succeeded in making my gender irrelevant ... even to myself.

Discussions about women in game development heated up around the Internet. They heated up in my social circles, too, because after so many years in game development, most of my friends were fellow developers. The conversation erupted on Facebook, on Twitter, even in person. All of this was before #gamergate; that merely drove everything to the surface.

Why I'm Here

It's been a few years since I finally started talking about being a woman in games. The response—the backlash—is still the same. But I'm not. I'm different. Going through cancer and facing the potential outcomes gave me a laser focus on what matters to me. It helped me focus on why I believe that I'm here.

Before cancer, I never spoke about the issues women face in game development. And I do mean *never*. I chose to speak about what I did, about my areas of expertise, and make my gender irrelevant. I feel differently now, and here's why.

Ask yourself: Why am I here?

I would bet that many people reading this book, if you search your heart, believe you were meant to make games. It's one of the reasons you're here— not here, reading this book, but here on earth.

I know that's true for most game developers, because if we didn't believe that on a fundamental level, we wouldn't put up with so much crap to do this for a living. Yes, we "get to make games all day." We also get to work brutally long hours, have lower pay than other tech industries, have employers frequently go out of business, then have to relocate thousands of miles for work when they do ... that is, if you're not laid off when your game ships.

And women in game development get a bonus extra helping of crap. Some companies have stopped having credits in their games because women in the credits would find angry (or sometimes enamored) men searching them out on social media. A few women in the industry had attention go beyond that: receiving phone calls after being shown in a "Making of" video or even having anonymous packages sent to their homes.

That's on top of the daily slog through comments on your Twitter and Facebook feed every time there's a new article about the kinds of games women play, much less about genuine sexism in the field. And that, in turn, is on top of the crap women in tech get in general. It's true across the board—even women who want to talk about having a *great* experience in game development or tech are hounded, badgered, and even threatened when they speak.

That's something new. Being a woman in game development used to feel like being a lonely, lonely unicorn. Now you sometimes feel like that slaughtered, bleeding unicorn in *Harry Potter and the Sorcerer's Stone.*

When I see all the crap getting in the way of someone doing what they're here on earth to do, I get upset. I want it to stop. I want all the doubters and deniers and haters to get out of our way. I'll be honest; sometimes it fills me with rage.

Then I remember being diagnosed with cancer. I remember that first, awful, lost week. I remember that when we linger in anger, fear, and doubt—when we live in it—we're living in darkness.

I'm not saying we shouldn't speak out—we should, whether our experiences are good or bad. In fact, it's important to talk about all aspects of game development. What makes it great? What makes it terrible? What challenges do we face, both as women and in our areas of expertise?

I'm also not saying we shouldn't confront the bias and anger that spews out when we *do* speak. We can't just roll over. We have to meet that bias with data, with facts, and with a steadfast sense of calm that comes from that fact that *we know this.* We know what happened to us and what didn't. We know what games we play, and what games we make. We know what we're talking about.

But we need to talk about more than women's issues, and we need to do more than fight those battles. We can't let the darkness and fear and anger overwhelm us. It can't be our focus. Why?

Because every day matters. In fact, every minute matters. Our time is not infinite. How we spend our minutes is what defines us as people.

We can't let anger steal our purpose. We can't let darkness steal our minutes. We have to focus on making those minutes matter. We have to remember why we're here—what is our purpose?

I discovered in 1982 that my purpose is to make video games. When did it happen for you?

Endnotes

1. You can listen to the full segment here: http://www.npr.org/sections/money/2014/10/21/357629765/when-women-stopped-coding
2. Zinner, Jill, et al. "Game Development Salary Survey 2001." *Gamasutra*. 15 Jul 2001. Available at http://www.gamasutra.com/view/feature/131465/game_development_salary_survey_2001.php?page=2

13

Elizabeth LaPensée

Writer and Cultural Consultant: *Venture Arctic*

Designer: *Survivance, Tulalip Tribes: Connected to the Land: Gathering Native Foods, The Gift of Food, Invaders*

Contributor: *United Indian Students in Higher Education Youth Day, Aboriginal Youth Science Exchange Camp, Urban Native Youth Association, Native Girls Code, Skins Workshops, and Electa Quinney Institute for American Indian Education*

When I contextualize myself as a woman, I am Anishinaabekwe. I am both an Anishinaabe and Métis woman through my mother's family and Irish through my father's family. My central communities are urban Native (a term I usually use rather than Native American, American Indian, First Nations, or Indigenous). My family is from Sault Ste. Marie. I consider myself border-less like my mother and my family who never recognized the lines between Canada and the United States. My relations are buried on Sugar Island along St. Mary's River which runs between Michigan and Ontario. I live for stories about times when the water there was so strong that all the land was covered in a mist. My culture and my family are inseparable from my work in games. This influences how I see existing games, what I see in games as a space for expression, and how I position myself as a game designer, writer, and artist.

I grew up understanding from my mother that I'm already living in the post-apocalypse. For my communities, the world as we know it has already ended. Day-to-day I'm positioned within a colonial takeover that continues an agenda of genocide. My circles are close and they are strong, made mostly of other Native women whose voices have at times been silenced and whose life experiences call on us all to grow and stand up with hope for change for the next generations. Games offer a pathway to pass on teachings and to strengthen intergenerational relationships, but we need our communities directly involved to make this happen.

Working around Colonial Design

I enjoy games, but most are inherently colonial in design. While I'm con-cerned with how Native people are represented in games—which often comes down to stereotypes—I'm even more concerned about mechan-ics and the insidious way games encourage behaviors of colonization. These games reinforce colonial thinking and often include mechanics that emphasize controlling, taking without replenishing, and competing against other players for personal gain. For example, land in real-time strategy (RTS) games is represented in maps that are marked based on ter-ritories. Often, land that has not yet been walked is blacked out, making everything exist in relation to the player and the perceived accomplish-ments of ownership and dominance. In contrast, I would like to see an RTS that represents the land as living and recognizes the connectivity of water, minerals, plants, and animals.

When playing an RTS, when playing most games, I eventually get burnt out because I'm not given ways to live my worldview through them. *Never Alone*, which was developed in collaboration with the Cook Inlet Tribal Council, has given me hope by using mechanics such as wind that can be a force against you or with you. However, this kind of gameplay is still rare.

In *Minecraft*, I want to be able to plant trees and plants and not just constantly take, take, take. In *Darkwatch*, I want to play as Tala, an empowered and determined woman. In *Turok*, I really just want to kick some ass with the Tek Bow instead of watch a storyline about a white man teaching a Native man how to be Native.

The moment I tried to work in the commercial game industry, I realized I didn't quite belong. My best experiences were with a community of game writers. We had our own support network and I always felt safe at events with them. But I quickly ran into women with horror stories, like being expected to go to strip clubs for work meetings. I was offered jobs I had to turn down because I couldn't be in an office culture where I would be teased about not drinking along with the guys. I've never gotten drunk because I've experienced alcohol's intergenerational damage, but I don't want to get into explaining that every time a situation comes up, so I just look like someone who won't play along. I'm grateful for friends I've found along the way who understood and wouldn't take that life choice personally.

Working from Within

Beyond the amazing writers, I was surrounded by men who, if they showed an interest in cultural representation in games at all, only wanted to benefit from the mystique of Native cultures without honoring protocol or the role of elders and storytellers in passing on vital teachings. Asking for input from communities didn't fit neatly in a production pipeline so the process was neglected. I had to step back from those games.

On the same note, there were games I started to be involved in and had to pull out from because my voice wasn't respected. I saw aspects of different cultures from all across Turtle Island being mixed up by designers and artists who didn't care about genuine representation. They just assumed they could take whatever they wanted from wherever they wanted, label, claim, and package it into a product to sell for their benefit with nothing going back to the communities they take from. Recognizing that I wasn't being listened to in those situations, all I could do was make sure my name wasn't on those particular games and move on in hopes of meeting people with interest in truly inclusive game development.

In 2007, I worked on *Venture Arctic* as a writer and cultural consultant. Thanks to my experience with Andy Schatz, who listened to and respected the input from community members and myself, I continued to believe games could be a space to engage players in Native perspectives through gameplay.

However, I branched away from the commercial game industry as a path and commercial games as a model. I needed a different approach that would actually reach Native people, even on reservations that have little to no Internet access. I've moved back and forth between living in cities and living out in the bush near a reservation, with long bouts of spotty Internet that couldn't handle Steam or massively multiplayer online (MMO) games. I don't see the point in making games that people I know can't play, which means I mostly haven't had strong enough Internet to work on large-scale games.

Outside of the Circle

To me, games are a way we can pass on teachings and language. Anishinaabemowin is a relational language, meaning nothing is simply an object, everything is in relation to something else. Games can be spaces for sharing place names, embedding stories in depictions of land, and interacting with mechanics that reinforce cultural values, just to name a few possibilities.

Despite my struggle with the tone of much of the game industry, above all else I enjoy games and believe in what they can bring to communities and especially what communities can bring to games. As a designer, writer, and artist (okay and occasionally a programmer), I do my best to uplift the perspectives of community members while working with all partners involved. Inclusive game development for me is about reciprocity and honoring the contribution of the people involved.

To this end, I've managed to make a living making games (also comics and animations) through alternative models to the commercial game industry. Sometimes, I still find myself negotiating from a place where I'm one voice serving as an advocate on a project, but mostly I've been fortunate enough to break away from those experiences by working directly with communities that invite me to walk alongside them for collaborative development.

While it can get stressful as a freelancer jumping contract to contract, this structure has been much healthier for me and my children. As a solo parent with only myself to rely on for financial and physical support (a role that's pretty common in Native communities), I've needed to bring my children along with me to meetings or have jobs that accept me working from home. I'm encouraged to see that, more and more, children are welcome at game industry events or increasing support is offered for parents, such as the Game Developers Conference now having childcare. It's a good indicator that the industry is starting to recognize the importance of balancing family and work. More support will naturally lead to more involvement from women who sometimes have to make a choice between their families and their jobs. Being the working parent has never been optional for me, and I'm grateful for people I have worked with who have understood that and embraced my children as part of the development process.

Self-Determined Games

Survivance[1] is a social impact game based on the Discovering Our Story project by Wisdom of the Elders and the Northwest Indian Storytellers Association. Development and playtesting took years of discussion and iteration because the game walks players through a journey of healing from historical and intergenerational trauma that results in acts of survivance—forms of self-expression inspired by Anishinaabe scholar and writer Gerald Vizenor's term meaning survival and endurance. In this game design, I especially liked the nonlinear gameplay. Players can choose any quest in any phase of the life journey based on where they are right then. The game shows players a path not just to survive but to thrive. Since development, the game has been played by urban Native communities who have later generated their own acts of survivance—including

Working Moms at Game Companies

Be aware that if you are the first person in your company having children, your pregnancy news is likely to be received with all the maturity of a class of fifth graders learning about menstruation. If your company has a lot of fathers working there, they may be more sympathetic, though only to a point—if most of the fathers have stay-at-home wives who take care of their kids, they may not understand why your situation would be different from theirs and have less empathy for your divided focus when you return to work.

If you are a mother looking for work in the game industry, or plan to start a family eventually, these are two of the biggest challenges you might face:

- *Crunch:* Game companies are used to employees who will work long hours on short notice, something that becomes difficult when you have a scheduled daycare pick-up, school vacations, and children's sick days to cope with. Talk to your superiors about your availability well before they ask you to work crunch hours—surprising them at the last minute when they're already strapped for time will go poorly for everyone.
- *Working from Home/Flexible Schedules:* Game companies vary tremendously in their support for remote work or flexible schedules. Although most game jobs can manifestly be done from home, at least sometimes, most companies prefer to have people in the office. And while many companies use some sort of "core hours" schedule to allow for flexibility, others have an official or unofficial policy of giving bonuses and promotions based on the number of hours they see you at your desk.

Editor

short films, animations, paintings, and prints—which are circulated through festivals and exhibitions.

Gathering Native Foods (2014) is a collaboration between the Oregon Museum of Science and Industry and the Hibulb Cultural Center. In this suite of touchscreen games, I wanted to see players slow down and think about the action of taking foods. For example, in the salmon-catching mini game, if a player takes more fish than the community needs for a feast, they are told they took too many. The tendency of players in touchscreen games is to rapidly tap the screen, but this mechanic requires them to consider their actions. Community members from the Hibulb Cultural Center also wanted players to see the differences between their traditional territories and the little their community is left with now; this was integrated into the menu interface. These games teach seasonal knowledge about land and traditional foods, and they have toured nationally in museums.

The Gift of Food (2014) is a board game that was created in collaboration with the Northwest Indian College. Initially, it was going to be a video game, but when community members shared that they didn't have regular computer access, the focus shifted to a board game that could be played in homes, community centers, and classrooms. My favorite aspects of the game include the seasonal gameplay; mechanics based on the values of collaboration, stewardship, generosity, and gratitude; and the fact that the winner is determined not based on how much food they have at the end of the game but rather on the diversity of foods in their food gift basket. From the art by Roger Fernandes to the depth of knowledge about plants, animals, and land, this game signifies to me the beauty of inclusive game development. The game is so strong at passing on traditional teachings that it is played only within the community and shared privately. I am honored to be part of a game that is fully self-determined and acts to protect knowledge.

Invaders[2] was just a blast to develop. It was exciting to take a step away from jumping contract to contract in my freelance life to work on a game entirely independently. *Invaders* is a web and mobile game inspired by the art of Steven Paul Judd, that plays on the classic arcade game *Space Invaders*. I bootstrapped it up and pushed myself to code with the help of friends. Similarly, Trevino Brings Plenty expanded his skills to create the game music. We had no funding and I didn't put a price tag on it. It's a giveaway. To date, it's the most downloaded game made by an all-Native team. It's also been circulated through festivals and exhibitions.

Artwork from Invaders, *2015. Design and Programming by Elizabeth LaPensée, Art by Steven Paul Judd*

Full Circle

In each of these games, I was empowered either by collaborating with other community members or by being listened to by people who respected my perspective. *Invaders* and *Survivance* are the only games I've worked on that have had an entirely Native team. While this isn't absolutely essential to making games with Native themes, my hope is that more and more community members will have the self-determination to create their own games … with the caveat that Native people shouldn't be expected to *only* make games with Native themes.

Because what each person creates should be up to them, whatever they may want to express, in whatever way.

Endnotes

1. http://www.survivance.org, 2009–2011.
2. http://www.survivance.org/invaders/, 2015.

14

Elizabeth Sampat

Senior Game Designer: *Tom Clancy's Ghost Recon: Commander, Home Design Story, Dream Life, Castle Story, Kingdom Clash, Plants vs. Zombies 2*

My very first salaried position in the industry was at a Fun Company™. It was very important to the higher-ups that we understand that our company was a Fun Company. There was beer on tap, meetings happened in beanbag circles, and on Friday there would be wine tastings with fancy hors d'oeuvres. It was a strange mix of cruise ship, kindergarten, and testing procedure specification (TPS) reports.

The focus of this Empirical Fun was the slide.

There was a fire-engine-red spiral slide that connected the first and second floors; at the time, this was the peak of start-up chic. No one ever used it, though. It turned out that when the company moved into the building and decided to install the slide, they accidentally installed it upside-down.

Now, the beginning of the slide was smooth and straight, and the bottom was twisted and fast and actually hazardous for your health. Instead of paying to reinstall the slide, they simply put beanbags at the bottom and required all employees to sign a liability waiver. The appearance of fun was more important than the *presence* of fun, even if it meant causing bodily harm.

I think a lot about that slide when I think about existing as a woman in our industry. We're in games, right? Games are fun. They should be fun. Making them, therefore, should be fun. And that's how it appears from the outside: glossy, childlike, exciting. But when you get closer, you realize there's something fundamentally wrong; the thin veneer of fun masks something more dangerous.

And no matter how fun it looks from the outside, you're the only one who's liable if you get hurt.

Breaking In

I came to the game industry in a circuitous way. I'd been a professional photographer for 10 years when I moved to the sleepy college town of Northampton, MA, to be closer to Internet friends after a failed marriage. These were people that I knew from a forum on creative writing, but they all happened to be tabletop game designers. I'd help playtest their role-playing games (RPGs) every week, and every week they'd ask when I was going to design something to bring to the group.

I always politely declined. "My brain just doesn't work that way." The cognitive bias against women in games is strong. I grew up playing tabletop RPGs, I'd made a ton of fan material for my favorites, but *even with encouragement* I could not picture myself as a game designer—in large part because so few game designers looked like me.

Fortunately, my friends were assholes who didn't take no for an answer. Eventually, I made a quick little game called *It's Complicated* for my roommate's birthday. We played it on occasion, and I thought I was done. But, as I mentioned, my friends were assholes.

Not only was I cajoled into designing my first game, I was then cajoled into self-publishing it. After I'd ordered the first print run, my friends Vincent Baker and Ben Lehman told me I was going to sell it at GenCon, the largest and oldest tabletop game convention in the United States. They even went so far as to split the cost of my booth space, and I owe them for everything that happened after.

I was working the Saturday morning shift at GenCon when a silver-haired man rushed in as soon as the doors opened, plopped down a $20, and said "I'm here to buy *It's Complicated* by Elizabeth Shoemaker.[1]" I introduced myself and handed him a copy of my game, surprised anyone had heard of it. He said he'd been following the development closely on my blog, and asked if I'd considered making digital games instead—my sensibilities seemed like they'd translate nicely. He told me his name was Ryan, handed me his card, and walked off like the happy customer he was.

"Do you know who that was?" a friend at the booth asked me.

"He said his name was Ryan."

That's when I learned the man was in fact Ryan Scott Dancey, creator of the D20 Open Game License, developer of *Dungeons and Dragons 3.5*, and the then chief marketing officer of CCP Games. I stared at the $20 bill he handed me, and realized he might have made that money creating the game I'd played so much in high school. That kind of validation, less than a year after I'd designed the first draft of a game I assumed no one would ever play, broke my brain. I couldn't stop staring at the money in my hand. Andrew Jackson just stared back at me like I was an idiot.

That's when I decided I was going to work in video games.

Breaking Down

I'm still not sure how my family survived the next few years. I took whatever freelance gigs I could get, the most lucrative of which was a long stint as a search engine optimization (SEO) spam writer. I wrote 40,000 words a week for $500 a week under the table, and it was the most money I'd made in my whole life. I spent one Thanksgiving at my fiancé's parents' house, writing 20 400-word "articles" about adult diapers, then came home to find that we were out of heating oil and it was 10 degrees below zero. I plugged in our little space heater, held my baby daughter to my chest for warmth, and the four of us huddled around until we were warm enough that it was safe for us all to sleep in the same room. The power company isn't allowed to turn off electricity for lack of bill payment when you have an infant in the house, and that's how we survived the harsh Massachusetts winter.

That and the money I made from the games I published.

Somehow I found the love and the time to keep making games. I existed in the cracks and breaths between faux-informational articles about why you should invest in gold and my daughter's diaper changes. I released two more tabletop RPGs, obsessively googled "how to break into the game industry" and tried to follow all of the advice I found. Eventually, a game designer I admired deeply discovered me: Brenda Romero (Chapter 2). She made a joke on Twitter about how the two of us made up half of all of the women designing board games in the world and started following me. Eventually, she saw me tweet about how I wanted to transition into digital games, and asked if I'd be willing to relocate. She made some introductions, and that's how I ended up at the company with the red spiral slide.

I went from food stamps to a job making more than my parents made together in small-town Montana, and it was doing something I loved: making games. I've never been so overwhelmed with gratitude in my life. I felt unworthy, despite the years of hardship and sacrifice that I'd put in to get to the point where I was lead designer on my own digital game. In hindsight, I think this is why so many women developers can seem cold and hard; too much gratitude and impostor syndrome make you an easy target for anyone who wants to exploit you.

My product manager scheduled an 11:15 a.m. meeting for the two of us, every Wednesday, in which he would stand less than a foot from me while yelling about how useless I was. He physically held his hand over my mouth on conference calls. My boss would play *Angry Birds* on her phone and ignore his behavior. At one point, the first time I was left alone with a writing contractor, he immediately made a joke about raping me.

I cried myself to sleep every night, bewildered by my life, guilty for feeling homesick for a world in which I worked 16-hour days and was still unable to provide for my children. *This is the reward for all of my hard work?* I asked myself. *This is the career I sacrificed everything for?*

And every morning I dried my tears and went back to the office with the red spiral slide.

Breaking Out

A few months into my tenure, the company's dysfunctions led to an implosion. I left the company for new opportunities a mere week before a third of its employees were laid off. My next job—working at Brenda Romero's company—could not have been more different.

I was hired as co-designer on a social game, working for a man named Tom Hall. Tom was kind and supportive, and he was also the mastermind behind my childhood favorite game series, *Commander Keen*. I used to say that working for my childhood idol was like being six years old and having Neil Armstrong show up at your door and ask if you want to go to the moon.

It was easy to flourish in the weird little utopia that was Loot Drop. The gender ratio for game designers was 1:1, the company was small and familial, and every interaction between co-workers was grounded in fundamental respect for one another. I'm not sure I would have stayed in the game industry if I didn't get a year's respite at such a unique company; I don't know if I would have been able to stomach it. There were no Nerf guns, and we had potlucks more often than catered lunch. Everyone worked hard, worked quietly, and went home to their children at a reasonable hour.

When I got laid off, my boss had tears in his eyes. I thanked Tom for everything he'd done for me, and everything that the previous year had been to me: a shelter and a place to grow. Then I packed up and left. I dropped by the office a few times after that—to bring food when the skeleton crew that remained couldn't leave, or to give advice. More than any other place I've worked, Loot Drop was family. I'm as grateful for the time I spent there as I am for that layoff. My company was safe, and nurturing, and I was so very comfortable. I would have stayed there, doing the same job and working under more senior designers, for my entire career. Instead, I was given an opportunity to grow that I never would have taken for myself.

No matter what's happened to me in the game industry—that abusive first job, getting laid off for the first time, Gamergate—I've never been able to shake off that intense feeling of gratitude.

Breaking Through

Despite this, "ungrateful" is one of the most common words used to describe me online—mostly by people upset when I constantly call out the game industry for being racist and sexist, and games culture in general for being hostile to women. "How can you hate the industry so much when it's done so much for you?" "Why do you have to ruin everything with your negative attitude?"

I believe we have a responsibility to the things we love, even if those things do not love us back. I am so grateful for the opportunities and experiences I've had in my four years in games; that gratitude specifically requires something to be grateful *to*. I am grateful to the game industry, and I express that gratitude by trying to change the industry—to make it better for everyone, and more welcoming to new people, new ideas, and new perspectives.

I told you about how I got here: the sleepless nights, the abject poverty, my single-minded passion and drive to make games. And that's a great story. It's the kind of feel-good movie that stars an actress who hasn't quite reached "household name" status but is gunning for a Golden Globe anyway. The thing is, that story is a lot less inspiring when you're living it.

Here's what I want for the game industry: I want self-taught women developers to never have to do what I did in order to get their first shitty game job. I want women to feel respected and supported wherever they end up, whether it's at a quiet family-oriented company like Loot Drop or a Fun Company with a slide. I don't want existing as a woman in the game industry to be any more remarkable than existing as a woman in dentistry, or accounting.

I don't want to be special or unique or exceptional. I want to be mundane.

I'm Out of Breaking Phrases Now, Actually

Despite (or partly because of) my inauspicious beginnings and outspoken nature, I have the best job of my career right now. I work for a company called PopCap on the franchise *Plants vs Zombies*, and I get to make silly, beautiful, challenging content that will be played by millions of people every day. When I interviewed for this position, one of the producers asked me the question every company asks every potential new hire:

Why do you want to work here? *Why PopCap?*

I answered by showing him a picture of my kids on Halloween, four years ago.

My Kids, Halloween 2011

It's funny: as a parent, you always want your kids to be proud of you. You want to impress them. Nothing makes you feel as human and fallible as having total responsibility for small humans who tend to think of you as godlike and perfect, even when you try your best to show them otherwise. So when I got a job working on my kids' favorite franchise, I came home with rock-star swagger.

But because my kids are *my daughters*, I can't just let my story end there. I can't climb up to the "No Girls Allowed" treehouse and push the ladder down behind me. When I see my 12-year-old making text adventure games in her spare time, or my 6-year-old comes to me with detailed drawings of new plants or zombies she wants to see implemented in my game, that rock-star pride mixes with cool, abject terror.

What if my daughters want to be like me when they grow up?

We tell our daughters they can be whatever they want to be, and it's like guiding them through a posh department store where none of the items have price tags. We're so afraid to dash their hopes and dreams with talk of the Real World, or the actual cost of getting everything you want. There's a tension between empowering my daughters and preparing them, and I constantly worry that I'm erring too much toward one side or the other.

And when I am in that moment, torn between concern and support, I realize that the things I want for the game industry are the same things I want for my children.

Endnote

1. My name at the time.

15

Erin Hoffman-John

Designer: *Go Pets: Vacation Island, Kung Fu Panda World, SimCityEdu: Pollution Challenge, Argubot Academy,* and many others

I've always been a resonator. Usually an unconscious one. That's what ea_spouse was about.

A few years ago, the gaming and game development communities were experiencing the foreshocks of what would become Gamergate in 2014. And, possibly because I am a resonator, I was headed for a full-tilt psychological breakdown.

It happened in harmony with the game community's fracture, the quieter breaking point that happened just prior to Gamergate. Gamergate hit like a 10.0, but there were foreshocks, some of them bad enough (you can google

ea_spouse

There are lots of things you can read about my experiences as "ea_spouse" on the Internet, enough that it's hard to know what to say about it for this book. The history goes something like: I was going to be a philosophy PhD, but got a job in games instead. I recruited my fiancé to the company that hired me. That company imploded. My fiancé got hired by EA in a talent sweep. We had one of the hardest years of our lives. I wrote a blog post.[1]

I worked in games the whole time.

People often ask whether things have gotten better. In reality, they ebb and flow. It tracks with the stock market. In boom times we talk about quality of life and intelligent work practices. In times of hardship, developers, like all laborers, become easier to abuse. What I would say is that we *are* laborers; we are the production line. Any argument otherwise has its origins with the bean-counters to whom it is a great advantage for laborers not to realize what they are and the power that they have.

Some of the biggest changes have happened where things had been the worst, which, in pure systems balance terms, must be generally true; some of these places were either going to improve or explode. And yes, there was a bit of drama when I came to my current job … at GlassLab, a nonprofit hosted on the EA campus. I will say that I've met amazing people here, and it's a radically changed place. I put the credit for that on the shoulders of the people here who saw the need for change and made it. It's a far larger accomplishment than any one person could lay claim to, and it is remarkable. So too is GlassLab itself—the reason why I'm here. I encourage anyone reading this to look into our work and maybe drop me a line. I like to think we're using games to change the world for the better.

"dickwolves," but bring a helmet) that a colleague and friend asked me to be a bridge-builder, to come and speak at PAXDev about healing the community. The panel was called "Harassment in Games." It was 2012, and we had no idea what lay ahead.

I went to dinner with a host of new friends. They were intimidating and wonderful—and full of prescriptions for what I should say on this panel. I was terrified. I ate very little, went back to my hotel room early, and, instead of going to sleep, began the first of what would become two weeks straight of chained panic attacks. (The clinical term for this, I would learn, is "acute panic disorder." I was pretty sure at the time it was some kind of cancer or actual insanity. I would spend the next several years in treatment for it, but that's another story.)

Mid-attack, I wrote the essay below, and e-mailed it to my colleague the following morning in lieu of appearing on the panel, claiming food poisoning.

On Harassment in Gaming

I remember the exact moment when I learned about sexism: what it is and how it works. I was in sixth grade, and I played football. I played football because I enjoyed it, I was good at it, and because my parents didn't believe in telling a little girl that some things aren't allowed, so I didn't know that I wasn't supposed to.

I liked it so much that I wanted to play outside of school. My friends played Pop Warner, the only kids' football league—in which I was allowed to be a cheerleader, but not a football player.

I took this issue to my dad, the arbiter of justice in my world. I said, "But I'm good at football, Dad. I'm better than the boys at it." (This was true. Boys bringing new boys into our lunch recess game would take them aside, point at me, and say "Don't treat her like a girl. She'll kill you.")

And then my dad said something to me that it must have killed him to say: "Honey, *it doesn't matter how good you are*. They don't let girls play. You're right, everything you say is right, it isn't fair—and I'm sorry."

I remember the very physical way the incredulousness and rage filled my small body. I was literally shaking with anger and disbelief. It wasn't about football. Everything I had been told about my world was wrong—that you can be anything you want to be, that with hard work anything is possible, that the world rewards excellence. It was all bullshit.

I was beginning down a path that ultimately leads many women to ardently identify as feminists. But I was too young to understand this, and instead of being able to conclude that the *world itself* was wrong, I did something darker, simpler, and more childlike.

In that moment, two things happened: one, I cursed in front of my father for the first time; and two, I stopped being a girl.

So profound was my disbelief at this injustice—and so great my stubbornness—that I turned away from everything feminine. I became officially a tomboy. And I set out to prove that not only would I be a tomboy, I would out-boy any boy set before me. I would be the *best* boy.

But something else happens when you abandon all girly things. If you are in middle school, you get kicked out of being a girl.

It isn't clear or direct, because few things about girls are. You get pushed aside; they tell you with subtle body language, with the absence of their praise, with all-in-fun teasing that is not all-in-fun. They kick you out. At 35, as a professional who now works regularly with middle schoolers, I understand it. At that age, boys and girls are beginning to really internalize what it means to be one gender in society. Things are changing slowly—those definitions are steadily evolving outside the binary—but when I was growing up, the differences were stark and absolute. You can behave in certain specific ways—or you can get kicked out.

From that point on, I hated girls. I didn't hate specific girls, but I hated the concept of what a girl was. I hated pink. I hated shopping. I hated curly hair.

And deep down, I hated myself.

This lasted me through middle school, through high school, well past college. I was very functional. In fact I was highly functional: gifted classes, then AP, college scholarships, student leadership. There were other things I was good at and loved that, as a girl, I was not supposed to love—biology, computers, science fiction, and video games.

Geek Culture

I was a geek, something that, when I started college in 1999, was just beginning to find mainstream acceptance. I went to a college that was over 75% male. My few female friends—all tomboys also—were online only. All of my meatspace friends were guys.

But in geek culture I found my people. For the first time, I really (*really*) seemed to belong somewhere. I could talk about *ToeJam and Earl* or genetics or HTML and get enthusiastic replies, or a spirited argument, which was just as good.

I had been making video games for approximately three years before I realized that making video games was a career choice. I worked on them for free because that was what I loved—and because I was good at it. People still told me that a girl wasn't supposed to do these things, but by then, I'd gotten used to brushing that off. I'd internalized it as normal. And part of me quietly knew that since I wasn't a girl anyway, since I'd been kicked out, proper girl things were not available to me.

Making games professionally would turn out to be substantially more complicated than I or my friends could have imagined.[2] But despite the long hours and the canceled projects and the setbacks and the struggles, I remained loyal to video games and what they represented. These were my people—the only people in my life who fully accepted and understood me. I defended video games against all comers: the press, my extended family, my father (who was often horrified by the violence in console games).

The argument for video games then—from about 2004 to 2009—was, and remains, on the side of the angels: video games are about speaking science to dogma, about truth to power, about challenge and testing limits and heroism. They're about garages and truth and where the heart meets the brain. I believe this still. When the mainstream accused video games of making children violent, we stood up and said no—the science says no. Video games do not make humans into monsters.

But as time went on—as video games grew and split and formed new subgenres, as I had to take a stand against console gamers on behalf of MMO gamers, then casual gamers, then social gamers—and as video game culture seemed to grow ever more violent, more negative, more dark ... something was changing in me, too.

Becoming Yourself

As I grew and gained confidence, I began questioning my assumptions (as any true devotee of science would do). I moved beyond an abstract understanding of the need for diversity and equality—still thankfully non-controversial concepts—and into questioning my now near-lifelong total rejection of all things feminine. I knew, because science had incontrovertibly declared it, that gender had no bearing on intelligence or academic achievement; so I started to wonder why there were still so few women in the geek community, if we stood for what I thought we stood for.

I started asking these questions out loud, and in print. Slowly, I started unpacking my knee-jerk rejection of Girl Things. And I found the hatred, I found the self-loathing, I found the betrayal and despair that had filled me as a child, which, in the way of childhood things, had grown with me and now consumed this place inside me that was large and dark.

So I did what any good geek would do: I started fighting it with science. I started asking hard questions. I started wearing makeup.

Bit by bit over the last five years I have been leveling up my girl skills. It's hard. Things that most girls began absorbing when they were 10, I have had to awkwardly learn as an adult—and often from women who were aghast at my ignorance, whose criticism I feared, irrationally, more than nearly anything else.

But then something else happened. As I started asserting this part of myself—not with argument, but simply by expanding who I was—I found resistance.

It wasn't comprehensive—it wasn't *all* of my guy friends—but it was enough. And it wasn't hate or overt attacks. It was subtle, and almost certainly unintentional. It was an "ew, gross" laugh if I talked about shoes or clothing. It was a "what!" of surprise if I was going out to buy makeup. And sometimes it was a more direct, "but you're not one of those girls."

They were trying to kick me out.

It turned out I wasn't actually as accepted as I thought I was. They weren't mean—they just didn't understand much about girl culture, and what they thought they understood, they didn't like. And when there was something worse—when there was an inappropriate comment from someone in the business, when there was hate speech on the Internet—they brushed it off because that's boy culture, and we are a boy culture.

I concluded quickly, as thousands of geek women have concluded, that if I put my head up and asserted what I was, I would be attacked by trolls. But none of us really care about trolls. What we care about is when our friends fail to stick up for us. When our friends refuse to understand or accept us. When we get kicked out.

Realizing this part of game culture has been like experiencing that childhood betrayal all over again. This community that was supposed to be about truth and excellence was really just Pop Warner redux. Be good ... but don't be better than the boys. You can be anything you want ... so long as what you want is to be exactly like us.

A Fight for Games

We are kicking out girl geeks. It's been happening for years. I haven't played a console game, really, since the PS2. Because I am getting the subtle, and sometimes not-so-subtle, message that what I am is not wanted.

What I want to fight for—what it would really kill me to lose—is what video games were supposed to be about. Was it all a lie? Are we really the preadolescent *Lord of the Flies* monsters that the mainstream has always said we are? As the harassment problem escalated, as it became, mind-bogglingly, a *debate* about whether it was okay for men to call women fat whores or stupid bitches on live game chat—as it became impossible to have a conversation about what those words mean and why we use them—as we became a culture where an indie game developer will create a game specifically intended to punish and silence a prominent girl geek—the gulf opened wider.

I thought that video game culture was about truth. That is what my culture is.

And the truth is even darker than we want to admit. The truth is that my self-loathing as a child, my abdication of my girlhood, was part of a long and winding pattern that makes stops at income inequality and descends into women being forced to bear children against their will, into women who are sold into slavery and stoned to death for appearing in public with a man not of their family. By abandoning the feminine in my life, I was participating in a cycle of terror that is ancient and still powerful.

I know I can't go back to the way I was. Even though I have made some amazing friends in the girl world, I can't go back to them, either, even if I turn my back on game culture for good. The ethical person in me wonders how I can stand this, how a good person can participate in a culture that specifically harasses women purely for being women. I have gone too far into the truth to be able to tolerate it much more.

But if I leave, I will be a person without a country. And so I continue to stick it out—in part because of the inspiration provided by the women who have stood up and made themselves vulnerable and been breathtaking in their fearlessness and poise. What they are doing is beautiful and brave and true.

So too is the transformation I am slowly seeing within my male friends and colleagues. We each go through this in our own way. I have tried to limit their exposure to my rage, to my own personal resistance, no matter how passionately I feel about it. Because at the end of the day my rage, however valid, is not an excuse to attack my friends.

All of this is why we need to seriously address this infection in our community. It isn't just about our friends or our sisters or our daughters. It is about the vitality of the culture itself. It is about either being a place where women have to pretend not to be women to get by, or a place that truly stands by its no-boundaries ethos. If we can't attack this problem with something more than half-hearted, "I guess we'll do whatever doesn't cost us anything or expose us to criticism" measures, we are going to lose what was greatest about game culture. We are going to lose the truth.

What It's Like

being a woman in games
   is ginger rogers backwards in high heels.

it's an echoing empty women's restroom
   and that moment you couldn't take it anymore
   memorialized in linoleum, bleach, lemon floor cleaner.

it's a forty-six-year-old man telling you you're not a normal woman
   and he knows what normal women want.

it's the threat of being the angry dangerous young woman
   the threat of being the hot, smart chick who might turn you down
   the threat of being the marriageable employee
      the threat of being the resource who might have a baby
      the threat of being the one who might sue you for your bullshit
      the threat of being too old to give a fuck anymore

it's being a threat at any age
it's a thousand reasons to hire a replaceable white dude
it's having to answer the question
    "what is it like to be a woman in games?"

Endnotes

1. Editor's Note: Erin's "ea_spouse" blog post took on the topic of crunch in the game industry. Its condemnation of crunch and the cost for game industry families struck a nerve and turned into a groundswell of protest. Ultimately, two class-action suits were filed against Electronic Arts, which led to EA paying out $14.9 million to programmers and $15.6 million to artists for previously unpaid overtime. For further information, see Surette, Tim. "EA Settles OT Dispute. Disgruntled 'Spouse' Outed." *Gamespot*. 26 Apr 2006. Available at http://www.gamespot.com/articles/ea-settles-ot-dispute-disgruntled-spouse-outed/1100-6148369/

2. For further thoughts from Erin about her early days in game development, see "Cyberpunked: The Fall of *Black9*" (http://www.escapistmagazine.com/articles/view/video-games/issues/issue_146/4814-Cyberpunked-the-Fall-of-Black9) and her original ea_spouse post, "The Human Story" (http://ea-spouse.livejournal.com/274.html).

16

Don't Girls Hate Combat?
Variety in Game Design

Gary Gygax, creator of *Dungeons & Dragons* (and therefore the creepy old grandfather of all role-playing games and much of the video game industry), once famously said "Gaming in general is a male thing .... Everyone who's tried to design a game to interest a large female audience has failed."[1] For many years, even as games like *The Sims* broke all sales records and drew a 60% female audience,[2] Gygax's attitude was common in the video game industry, with game designers assuming that girls just "didn't like" combat or rules or vigorous system design and were therefore unsuited to design games.

Needless to say, this was always based far more in prejudice than fact. Women have made strides in design. Though still only representing 13% of all designers,[3] women can and do occupy prominent design roles on combat-heavy, male-focused games (the granddaddy of all massively multiplayer online [MMO] Battle Arenas, *League of Legends*, has the remarkable Christina Norman as lead designer[4]). And the recent explosion in game genres ensures that even if corridor-based shooter levels aren't your cup of tea, there is room in the game industry for your particular talents.

Game Genres

This is an incomplete list of the types of game genres currently popular, showing the great variety in design skills needed in the industry. Most of the genres below will require one or more of the following types of designers (titles and responsibilities will vary greatly from company to company): combat designers, gameplay designers (for noncombat gameplay), system designers (who balance the numbers behind the game systems), puzzle designers, level designers (who plan maps and encounters), quest or mission designers (who plan story and gameplay for individual missions and may also write dialogue), cinematic designers (who stage interactive dialogue gameplay), monetization designers (who plan how free-to-play games will engage players enough to spend money), and user experience designers (who ensure that the user interface and gameplay experience engage players).

- *Shooters:* Gameplay is primarily gun-related combat.
- *Action/Fighting Games:* Gameplay is primarily melee combat or a mix of melee and gunplay.
- *Role-Playing Games (RPGs):* Gameplay is a mix of combat, exploration, character customization, and other systems.
- *Adventure Games:* Gameplay is a mix of exploration and puzzles, possible minor combat.
- *Sports Games:* Gameplay simulates popular sports.
- *Racing Games:* Gameplay is driving and customizing vehicles.
- *Platformers:* Gameplay is climbing and jumping on things, *Super Mario* style.
- *Hidden Object Games:* Gameplay is clicking on hidden objects in scenes to advance a story.
- *Endless Runners:* Gameplay is racing endlessly through different levels, sometimes with combat.
- *Building Games:* Gameplay is the construction of new objects from objects in the game.
- *Strategy Games:* Gameplay is building armies and engaging in large-scale warfare.
- *Sim Games:* Gameplay simulates real-world activities such as running a city or company.
- *Dating Sims:* Gameplay simulates romantic relationships.
- *Educational Games:* Gameplay may be anything, but the game goal is to teach a lesson.
- *Preschool Games:* Gameplay is tapping or clicking in a way preliterate kids can do alone.

Becoming a Game Designer

Game designers need a mix of technical and creative skills, and may lean more to one side than the other, depending on the company and personal preference. Most design positions require[5]

- *Programming:* The majority of designers have some programming background, either through schooling or self-taught.
- *Previous Design Experience:* Until recently there was no formal schooling path available to aspiring designers, so most refined their design skills in modding communities or at game jams. But many colleges do now offer a game design program, which allows up-and-coming designers to perfect their skills with faculty mentors.
- *Extensive Gaming Experience:* For designers, even more than other disciplines, it is crucial to play a lot of games. Designers must be familiar with what is on the market and be able to study competing games with an eye to what did and didn't work.
- *Good Writing and Communication Skills:* Game design is a collaborative process, and designers are often the keepers of the vision (for the game or for a specific level) and must be able to communicate that vision to all departments through their documentation.
- *Many Interests:* Games are made about a huge variety of topics and settings, so designers with broad interests have a leg up if they can go into an interview and already be an expert on anything from *Star Trek* to feudal Japan.
- *Understanding of Current Game Market:* Most designers these days will find that designing monetization into the core game is an important responsibility.
- *Sense of Fun:* Designers more than anyone else are responsible for making the game *fun*.

For Allies

Just as their skills straddle "hard" technical expertise and "soft" creativity, female designers can expect to face both hard and soft sexism. Since design is a more subjective field than programming, it can be harder to define a "good" designer. This opens the field to a plethora of unconscious biases, from condemning female designers who prefer less mainstream games ("How can she make a popular game if she doesn't even like *Game of War?*"), to assuming that a collaborative workstyle means a candidate won't stick to her guns. ("She was such a pushover. Why did she take all of my suggestions?")

Most of the suggestions for programmers (Chapter 8) apply for designers, too. Gender-blind hiring, anonymous reviews, and mentoring are all important steps toward helping your company attract and retain female designers.

Starting a Game Company as a Designer

Many designers enter the field with a strong vision for the game they want to make. This is unlikely to happen within a large corporate structure (where games are often greenlit by committee, not driven by a vision), so many designers found indie studios to make the kinds of games they want. This brings female designers into a position to face still more gender bias, as studies have shown that only 15% of venture-capital-backed new companies had a woman on the executive team, and only 2.7% had a female CEO.[6] If you are going this route, it is wise to find a partner whose expertise is the money side of the business. It's a lot to ask of yourself to be a brilliant designer, a competent programmer, and have an excellent head for business.

Endnotes

1. Wilson, Steve. "RevolutionSF Remembers Gary Gygax: Sex, Drugs and D&D." *RevolutionSF*. 5 Mar 2008. Available at http://www.revolutionsf.com/article.php?id=3964
2. Huguenin, Patrick. "Women Really Click with The Sims." *New York Daily News*. 15 Apr 2008. Available at http://www.nydailynews.com/life-style/women-click-sims-article-1.283191
3. "Gamasutra's Annual Game Developer's Salary Survey." 2015. Page 3. Available at http://www.gamesetwatch.com/2014/09/05/GAMA14_ACG_SalarySurvey_F.pdf
4. Alexander, Leigh. "Former Mass Effect 2, 3 Lead Gameplay Designer Joins Riot Games." *Gamasutra*. 12 Jul 2011. Available at http://www.gamasutra.com/view/news/125737/Former_Mass_Effect_2_3_Lead_Gameplay_Designer_Joins_Riot_Games.php
5. For a good (if old) article on getting hired as a game designer, see Arnold Hendrick's "Hiring Game Designers." *Gamasutra*. 20 Mar 1998. Available at http://www.gamasutra.com/view/feature/131669/hiring_game_designers.php
6. Brush, Candida. "Diana Report, Women Entrepreneurs 2014: Bridging the Gap in Venture Capital." Arthur M. Blank Center for Entrepreneurship, Babson College. Sep 2014. Available at http://www.babson.edu/Academics/centers/blank-center/global-research/diana/Documents/diana-project-executive-summary-2014.pdf

17

Jennifer Brandes Hepler

Writer/Instructional Designer: Multiple parenting-related simulations for Kognito Inc.

Lead Writer: *Game of Thrones Ascent, Dream Weddings*

Senior Writer: *Dragon Age: Origins, Dragon Age II, Dragon Age Inquisition, Star Wars: The Old Republic*

Story Consultant: *The Unavowed*

In 1986, I was in fifth grade. My teacher was Matthew J. Costello, who in 1993 would go on to write *The Seventh Guest*, the horror adventure game that exploded CD-ROM gaming into the mainstream. Looking at a smart, nerdy, fantasy-loving little girl, his advice at my parent-teacher conference was, "Jennifer should find people who play *Dungeons and Dragons*. That's her crowd."

It would be another six years before I left my small town and could follow that advice.

I wanted to be a writer for as long as I can remember. Even as a toddler, I made up my own nursery rhymes, and by high school I was determined to "break in" before I graduated. I went to cons, met editors, and wrote away (back in the pre-Internet days) for submission guidelines for the magazines I followed. I wrote and submitted short stories all through high school, with predictable lack of success.

Then, when I arrived at the Johns Hopkins University, I finally met those D&D-playing guys I'd been looking for since I was 10. They were thrilled to meet a girl who wanted to learn role-playing games (RPGs) and immediately shoved a *Shadowrun* character sheet in my hand and yelled a lot of numbers, then threw some dice at me and told me to roll them. My takeaway from the whole experience was basically, "Huh?"

But a few weeks later, I picked up a *Vampire: The Masquerade* basic book, where it explained what had been missing from my garbled *Shadowrun* tutorial. The numbers on the page were *part* of the storytelling! They represented things about what the characters could do and how other people would react to them, and they determined the dice you rolled to make cool things happen.

I went back to the *Shadowrun* gamemaster (GM) (full disclosure—now my husband), and accusingly told him, "You never said the numbers on the page *meant* something!" He was floored, and many hours of discussion about ork birth-rates later, we had both begun our journey toward careers dedicated to making RPGs accessible for everyone.

Breaking In

After that rocky start, I fell in love with tabletop role-playing games, playing marathon sessions weekly all through college. The first RPG writing I did was for live action role-playing games, complicated sheets of history for every character. In 1996, I helped found JohnCon, the Johns Hopkins science fiction and gaming con, now in its 20th year (eek!). In the course of promoting JohnCon, I became a regular at Gen Con, Origins, and other tabletop gaming conventions. There, I ended up running demos and RPG tournaments for FASA Corporation, showing off the latest supplements for *Shadowrun* and its prequel, *Earthdawn*.

Ever one to keep my eye on the goal, I learned that volunteering to run the 8 a.m. Sunday morning demos when the developers were out drinking all night was a quick way into a gaming company's good graces! And my dedication finally paid off with two entries in the *Shadowrun* supplement "Threats." By the time I graduated college, I was working on my first full sourcebook for *Shadowrun*, "Cyberpirates" (written with Chris Hepler). I had also branched out to other games, working on *Earthdawn*, *Paranoia*, and *Legend of the Five Rings*.

Saving Throw for Half Cooties

My junior year of college, I did a term paper on gaming folklore, in which I was shocked to repeatedly hear in interviews that female players had their characters threatened with rape. It was a constant theme in my interviews with female gamers from the 1970s, 1980s, and 1990s. Keep in mind, these were not anonymous strangers on the Internet, but "friends" of the player, sitting in the same room as her.

This eventually turned into an article for *Shadis* magazine, called "Saving Throw for Half Cooties," my first official feminist gaming publication.

Six Years in Development Hell

Once I had to pay my own rent, I quickly realized tabletop games were not a viable career, so I picked the easy option—move to Los Angeles and break into TV writing! (Confession, I do not understand the word "easy.") The year after I arrived, *Survivor* came out, and the number of jobs in scripted television plummeted from the hundreds to the dozens overnight. After years of scraping by, I ended up on a show called *The Agency* in 2002 (the third, less successful CIA-themed show to air the same year as *24* and *Alias*), but when that gig ended, nothing else materialized.

After working on unproduced movie adaptations for several tabletop and video games, I took the plunge and went to the Game Developer's Conference (GDC) in 2005. My husband had been playing *Knights of the Old Republic* right before we left, and when we saw the BioWare booth with its big *KOTOR* poster, I turned to him and said, "Hey, that's that *Star Wars* game you've been playing. They seem to use a lot of words."

And thus do careers begin …

BioWare

With no idea of BioWare's reputation … or where Edmonton was on a map … I ended up talking to BioWare's Design Director, who wanted to

Maternity Leave (in the United States)

For many game companies, especially smaller ones, maternity leave policies aren't something they think to discuss before the day their first female employee announces, "I'm pregnant." This can sometimes lead to a scramble as companies who know nothing about standard maternity practices start trying to find an equitable solution. Unfortunately, for pregnant workers in the United States, there is little in place to let them preserve their careers while caring for their families.

The Family and Medical Leave Act requires only companies with more than 50 employees to provide maternity leave. Those who meet the requirement must provide only 12 weeks of unpaid time.[1] Different states have their own requirements. For example, California, where many game companies are located, requires any company with more than five employees to provide up to four months of leave,[2] while Texas, which also hosts many game studios in Austin, provides nothing beyond what is federally guaranteed.

When arranging maternity leave with a game company, it is important to know your rights beforehand. If your company has a human resources department, begin by talking to them, but be sure to tell your immediate supervisor yourself—you don't want them to hear your pregnancy news second-hand! Preparing a plan for how your responsibilities will be covered in your absence (and getting the buy-in from the co-workers covering those responsibilities!) goes a long way toward reassuring nervous companies.

Be sure also to explain your need for other missed time (for doctor appointments), the possibility of early labor or complications changing your careful schedule, and the need for any accommodations. Most game industry jobs are fairly sedentary, without much heavy lifting or other risk factors, but pregnancy is unpredictable and you never know when you might have to go on bed rest and work from home (or

hire both more women and writers with a Hollywood background. Since I fit both requirements, I sent in a writing sample, and some months later, my husband and I had to decide whether to move to the frozen north. I finally convinced him by pointing out, "We've lived in LA for six years and never been to the beach. We can probably drink hot chocolate and play RPGs just as well in Canada."

That was the best decision I ever made. I was put on the struggling *Dragon Age: Origins*, while my husband joined the *Jade Empire* team (and eventually ended up on *Mass Effect 2–3*). I created the Dwarf Commoner Origin in what was supposed to be a training exercise, but it became so beloved by the team that it made it into the game. I ended up writing all of the dwarf storyline and the first draft of the Landsmeet before going on maternity leave for my daughter's birth. When I came back to work, I was assigned to *Star Wars: The Old Republic*, where I got to play with a very different tone while writing the Smuggler. But when *Dragon Age: Origins* finally released to better-than-anticipated sales and reviews, the Dragon Age team wanted me back to help develop the sequel.

Pay Attention, This Is on the Test

At some point while on *Origins*, I did an interview for a short-lived women-in-games website called *Killer Betties*. One of the questions was, "What is the hardest part about being a game developer?" My response was "playing the game." I have visual perception issues that make game combat difficult for me, and as a mom, I have very little time to play. Since all I'm interested in is the story, I said I sometimes wished for a "fast-forward" feature that would let me skip the combat in games so I could play more of them. Remember this, it comes back in a big way.

run from an important pitch meeting to puke!). It is also wise to think about any accommodations you will need after you return to work, such as a private place to pump breast milk.

Editor

Dragon Age II

Dragon Age II was the most amazing work experience I've ever had. We had one year flat to make a BioWare game, something that generally took anywhere from three to six years. To hit our voice-over recording deadlines, the writing had to be done in under four months. The team came together like a dialogue-tree-vomiting Voltron and made every deadline … though the banter might show the effects of how punch-drunk we all were. There was little time for nitpicking, so every writer worked independently, leading to distinctive, memorable characters like Sheryl Chee's badass Isabella and Mary Kirby's hilarious Varric.

I desperately wanted to write a cursed, Buffy-and-Angel-style romance, which BioWare had never done before. That impulse turned into Anders, a rebel mage possessed by a spirit of Justice, which drives him to become a terrorist in the name of mage rights. Anders was intended to be a polarizing character, someone some players would deeply love and others righteously despise, and he has probably succeeded in being the most controversial character in BioWare history. (He was also, along with all DAII romances, romanceable by either gender, which means he might call your dude character handsome under certain circumstances. Strangely, some people objected more fervently to this than to him murdering a nun in order to start a religious war …)

The team was aware that we would get dinged in reviews for some of the shortcuts that let us make our release date (reused levels and lack of divergence in the ending being the biggest), but I, at least, had no idea what was in store.

In March 2011, I went to my brother's wedding. I was seven months pregnant and flying was awful. The morning after the wedding, I got up at the crack of dawn to fly home because *Dragon Age II* launched the next day and I wanted to be there for the celebration.

The day *Dragon Age: Origins* launched was a nonstop party. The entire studio was giddy as positive reviews poured in, the forums exploded with (mostly not negative for the whole first week!) comments, and the devs let out the breath we'd been collectively holding for six years. The launch of *Dragon Age II* could not have been more different.

Instead of a release-day party, the team sat in dead silence as vicious attacks on the game and on us came from every dark corner of the web. This was the day I learned the word "4chan," as their members slathered *Metacritic* with negative reviews and launched personal attacks, demanding the development team be fired.

Among other attacks on the team (including channers harassing an unrelated woman named Mary Kirby off of Facebook), someone found that old interview I did (told you this would come back). Since they disliked the changes that had been made to combat gameplay in DAII, they decided that because I didn't like combat, I must have become the lead combat designer and been responsible for the changes! (I also don't like sports. Do I run the NFL?) For the record, the only involvement I've ever had in combat design has been to submit bug reports that I was still dying on Easy mode.

There was a brief kerfluffle on the forums. A few people called for my resignation, others surprisingly agreed that a "skip combat" button, a cause I had long-since given up on, would drastically improve their gaming experience.

After a few days reeling over the negative reception, the team went back to work on DLC, and a few weeks later I went on maternity leave. Being in Canada, I had a full year off with my newborn son, and through the second half of 2011, the only association I had with gaming was occasionally trying to play *Dragon Age II* while my son was napping on my lap. (Strangely, he woke up every time I leveled up Fenris—I think he disapproved of how I spent my points.)

Many months later (Valentine's Day, to be exact), I got some strange messages from friends offering me support in this difficult time. I finally got one of them to answer what was happening—someone on Reddit had written a screed accusing me of being "the cancer that was destroying BioWare." I tried to laugh it off, but it went viral, and hundreds of people piled on with vicious Twitter comments. One or more frightening psychopaths wrote long rants in the BioWare forums saying he was going to hide in the bushes and kill my children on their way to school, because they should have been aborted at birth rather than go through life with me as their mother.

Even more frightening to me, as a Jewish woman, was that it took less than 48 hours for the misogynist attacks on me as a "fat bitch" to turn into neo-Nazi attacks on me as a "Jewess" who was taking over BioWare for the "Elders of Zion."

It was terrifying. I reached out to BioWare for help, and will always be grateful to founder Ray Muzyka for his swift and calm letter supporting me, which helped quiet some of the manufactured outrage. EA security took over the job of determining whether there were "actionable threats." I was fortunate in having the support of a large company—I didn't have to read most of the vitriol myself, because I trusted if someone was really coming to kill me, EA would probably send a memo.

I looked into a legal response, but ultimately decided that my last few months with my baby were irreplaceable, and I wasn't going to lose them fighting with jerks on the Internet. Instead, I shut down my Twitter account, unlisted my phone number, got bullet-proof glass on my windows, and went back to living my life. It was gut-wrenching to have to tell my daughter's kindergarten teacher to keep a special eye on her because someone who had never met her was threatening to kill her. (Because he didn't like a video game I worked on as much as he liked the *last* video game I worked on!) But thankfully, this was pre-Gamergate, and without celebrities working to keep the hate going, it died down quickly.

I went back to work at BioWare, writing the strong female character Cassandra Pentaghast, and continuing to advocate for making games more accessible and friendlier to new and casual players. I never stopped writing games, and I never stopped writing exactly the characters I wanted to write: male or female, gay or straight, strong or weak.

Conclusion

When I first wrote this essay, I struggled with how to end it. What is a satisfying conclusion to a life you're still living? I have been working as the lead writer on *Game of Thrones Ascent*, and greatly enjoying the chance to write original material for one of my all-time favorite fantasy stories. But just recently, a longtime interest I've had in serious games has come to a head, and in 2016, I am leaving commercial games to work for a company, Kognito Interactive, that uses interactive dialogue to train people in how to have more empathetic conversations, so they can become better doctors, teachers, and parents.

So what great lessons have I learned along the way? What wisdom can I impart to those of you who are hoping to pursue your own careers in games?

It was *Vampire: The Masquerade* that made me a gamer, and it was their Ventrue motto I've kept in mind throughout my career: *Outlive Your Enemies.*

Calm Parents, Healthy Kids an interactive learning simulation for parents. Kognito Interactive, 2016

When I faced those at-the-time-shocking levels of harassment, I ultimately decided that rather than fighting, I would best win by simply doing my job. I am a woman who writes games, who finds story more interesting than gameplay, who admits to having little time or energy to play games outside of work. I am a woman who achieved her dream of writing for a living, of sharing stories with an audience hungry for those stories. I am a woman who left a large and successful game studio with a hardcore audience and is using the skills she learned there to help real people in the real world.

And I think the right place to end my story is that I am here, working on something I love, at a job that allows me to care for my family in a way I feel good about, writing dialogue that will help players actually become better people, not just feel momentarily better about themselves. I am a woman, a writer, a mother, working in games. My life right now is pretty unremarkable, and that's kind of the point.

Endnotes

1. U.S. Department of Labor. "Family and Medical Leave Act." 1993. http://www.dol.gov/whd/fmla/
2. California Department of Fair Employment and Housing. "The California Family Rights Act." 2002. http://www.leginfo.ca.gov/cgi-bin/displaycode?section=gov&group=12001-13000&file=12940-12951

18

Sheri Graner Ray

Games: *Lexica, Puzzle Clubhouse, Battle Train, Daniel Tiger, Play It Forward–Elm Street Stories, Battle Ball, Triazzle, Tunnel Tail, Race for the Beach, GeoCommander, FusionFall, Wizard 101, CSI: Hard Evidence, Star Wars Galaxies: New Game Experience, Star Wars Galaxies: Trials of Obi Wan, Star Wars Galaxies: Roar of the Wookiee, Star Wars Galaxies: An Empire Divided, Nancy Drew: Secrets Can Kill, Nancy Drew: Stay Tuned for Danger, The Vampire Diaries, McKenzie & Co, The Lost Vale, Ultima VIII, Pagan, Arthurian Legends, The Ultima VII Part Two: The Serpent Isle, Ultima VII: The Black Gate*

Books: *Gender-Inclusive Game Design – Expanding the Market*

People often refer to me as an activist for women and games. Indeed, the first time I spoke on the subject was at SIGGRAPH in 1995, so I do have something of a history in that area. Because of this, one might expect me to talk about the "boys club" of the early game industry, how difficult it was being female, or about how it has changed in recent years. But truly, I see that as more of a hurdle than something that influenced me and my career.

When looking back, I realize the most influential decisions—the decisions that set me on the professional path to where I am today—occurred early in my life.

Dungeons & Dragons

My first actual contact with gaming came in 1981 when I was 20 and attending college. *Parade* magazine, a glossy supplement in the center of the Sunday newspaper, ran a cover story about a game called *Dungeons & Dragons*. While the article was not flattering, I was intrigued by a game that allowed players to experience adventures in a fantasy world. I asked around, but none of my friends had heard of it. So I took out an ad in the college newspaper looking for someone willing to teach me to play D&D.

Eventually, the younger brother of a high school friend volunteered to teach me and three of my friends. After the first session, I was hooked. We agreed to make this a weekly Saturday game and he left his books at my place. Every night I pored over them, reading the rules until the wee hours.

After a couple of weeks, our new Dungeon Master (DM) didn't show up for our scheduled game. I called his house and his mother told us that not only would he not be running our game that day, but he wouldn't be coming back anytime soon, as he had left to join the army.

I was devastated. I had found something in that game that touched me and I wasn't willing to give it up. I decided then that, if we were going to keep playing this game, I was going to have to run it. Armed with his *Dungeon Master's Guide*, his dice, and something called "Keep on the Borderlands—An Instructional Module," I set out to learn to run a role-playing game.

Soon, I had run through the small selection of modules our first DM had left with me. So, using the "Random Dungeon Generator" in the back of the D&D books, I built my own stories and adventures. This was the decision that started me on my game design career.

In 1985, my entire family moved to Austin, TX, and by 1989 I had a weekly game group running again. One night, as I had my players deep in an adventure, one of the group's henchmen was kidnapped. Through the evening of play, the group tracked their kidnapped friend to the lair of a demon. As the players crept deeper into the dungeon, they found themselves on a mezzanine looking down into a maze. There they saw evil creatures stalking their companion, playing cat and mouse with her. The group grew frantic, trying to figure out how to save her. Finally, one player shoved his chair back from the table, stood up and declared, "I can't watch this anymore," and stomped out of the room.

I can't *watch* this anymore.

Watch a game that was being played only in their minds. A game experience *I* had designed.

That was the moment it all crystalized for me. I realized what it was that made me love designing adventures for my players. When he pushed his chair back from the table that night, that player had not been sitting in my tiny, overcrowded kitchen. He had been deep in the lair of that demon, trying to figure out how to rescue his friend. I realized then that, with careful design, I could take my players away from their everyday world and transport them into a world of fantasy and adventure, a world where they were heroes. That, for me, was the magic. That was the rush.

Later that same year, a new member who'd been playing with us for about three months told me there was a job opening for a writer at his company. He said he thought I'd be a natural fit. I asked him what company it was and he said, "Origin Systems."

Origin Systems

I had never heard of Origin Systems. I didn't know much about computer games. I had played a few text adventures as a kid, but hadn't given much thought to how they were made. My friend assured me my experience writing my own adventures, adapting rule sets and such, made me a perfect candidate. I agreed to let him submit my resume and a few writing samples from the games I'd been running.

Four days later I got an interview. After being shuttled from office to office, talking to many people, I found myself sitting in Warren Spector's office. We hit it off and the next day, I got a job offer. Two weeks later, in 1989, I started at Origin Systems.

On my first day, as my new office mate gave me a tour, we ran into John Watson, one of Origin's first designers. He shook my hand and said, "Welcome to Origin. You'll never have to look for a job ever again."

While what John said was certainly not accurate, it was true in the sense that I had, indeed, found my home. I had found people who thought like me, had seen the same movies, played the same games, and read the same books. But most importantly, I had found people who had the same passion for creating the kind of gaming experiences that would take their players away from their regular life. I was home.

It was a magical time in gaming. There was no "industry" the way we think of it today. We didn't have licenses or properties. We had total creative freedom. How else could we make a top-selling game about someone called "the Avatar" who worked for "Lord British" and lived in a land called "Britannia"[1] ... and have it do well enough to warrant eight sequels!

We also had very little support or structure. Our development process, such as it was, consisted mostly of the daily whim of our producers. Nothing was written down. There were no design documents, no plans or schedules, just the producer coming in every morning and telling us what he wanted done or changed that day.

It was chaos.

I co-led a group of writers at Origin in a push to adopt something we called a "design blueprint." This was the forerunner of today's "design document." We envisioned this as something that would solidify our design and help keep the team focused. This, in turn, would help curtail the terrible schedule delays, crunch time, and budget overruns from which the company was suffering. Although there were cries of how this would "stifle creativity," the concept of this "design blueprint" was grudgingly accepted.

Women and Games

My interest in women and games also began during my time at Origin. In the *Ultima* series, when the player talked to a non-player character (NPC), a window opened showing a portrait of that character. These portraits were all based on real people. Usually it was us and our friends or family, but after a while we needed new faces. To solve this, we ran a contest where people could "win a chance to star in an *Ultima*" by sending their photo in with their game registration card.[2] We ended up with a big box of photos of our players.

At that time, I was working on a new game called *Arthurian Legends*. This game had a high percentage of female characters, so I grabbed the box of the contest entrants and started to pull out all the entries from women. I was amazed at how many we had. I asked if I could survey the female contestants. I argued that we could find out what they liked and didn't like and, using the information, expand our market. The box of photos was immediately taken from me and I was told, "(We) have more left-handed players than female players and (we) don't care what the left-handed players want. Why should (we) care about the female players?"

This was my first run-in with the "boys club." It could have stopped me right there. I could have nodded and quietly gone back to my job. That certainly would have been easier, but I couldn't. I had to know why women did or didn't play our games and what, if anything, they would want changed to make the games better for them. It didn't make sense to me that we would purposefully shut the door on a potentially huge market without at least a little exploration.

About that time, Electronic Arts bought Origin Systems and John's statement that I would never need to look for another job proved false. Shortly after the purchase, EA mandated a 30% across-the-board staff reduction and I was laid off. There were no other game companies in Austin at the time, and I ran into the hard fact that other technical companies did not consider game-development experience to be "real" experience.

This was another decision point in my career. Friends and family thought I was crazy for trying to stay in games. They told me while making games was fun, maybe a nice hobby, it was time to find a "real job." I think someone less stupidly stubborn than me would have become a bank teller and never looked back. There have been times I've thought that might have been the smarter choice!

American Laser Games

But I didn't give up. Building experiences that could take my players away from this world was my passion. I spent the next nine months working temp jobs while I figured out how to get back to making games. Between meager savings and lots of credit cards, I managed to make it to CGDC[3] as a volunteer. While I was there, a recruiter friend set up several interviews for me.

The interviews resulted in two job offers; one with Squaresoft and the other with American Laser Games.

I chose American Laser Games. This was a crossroad for me. I have often looked back and wondered what my career would have been like had I made a different choice.

At the time, American Laser Games was the last U.S. manufacturer of stand up arcade games. They were concerned about the increased Japanese domination of the arcade market and decided to start a new business division to diversify their business model. This group was called Her Interactive. The lure of working with the first development group in the United States dedicated specifically to making games for girls was too good to pass up. I accepted a producer/designer job, and in 1994 I moved to Albuquerque, New Mexico.

Now, during the interview with American Laser Games/Her Interactive, they told me they'd had a game in production for six months and they needed me to help "finish it up and get it out the door." Imagine my surprise when I showed up the first day and they pointed me to a box of developed movie film and a marked-up shooting script. This was sum entirety of their "game." Not a single line of code had been written. There wasn't even a team assigned to the product. I had three months to take this box of movies and turn it into a game.

But we did it. We pulled together as a team, and between many long nights of crunch, meals eaten out of Styrofoam boxes, and weekends of not seeing the outside of the office, we produced *McKenzie & Co.* The game sold 80,000 units over its lifetime, remarkable at a time when 100,000 units was considered a "blockbuster" title. The letters poured in from our fans, thanking us for making a game just for them.

Meanwhile, the U.S. stand-up arcade market had completely vanished. American Laser Games finally succumbed and declared bankruptcy. By this time, I had been promoted to Head of Product Development for Her Interactive and we were working on a licensed *Vampire Diaries* game. As I tried to keep the team together and the product on schedule, they were quite literally auctioning off the company around us. As assets were sold, we consolidated and moved until, at the end, we were down from 65 developers to 12. Our offices were closed off as the space was returned to the landlord. Finally all 12 of us, with our desks and computers, wound up crammed into the chief executive officer's former office.

Between trying to get the game out, worrying if the electricity would be shut off, and the uncertainty of even having a job, I wound up in the doctor's office with heart arrhythmia. After a full EKG and heart workup, the doctor walked in and looked at me. "Your heart is an innocent bystander of your brain," he told me. "It's not bad today, but if you don't find different work, you will land in some serious trouble in the future."

I didn't leave. I stayed another 18 months. In that time, we finished *Vampire Diaries*, the first Nancy Drew title, *Secrets Can Kill*, and began on the next Nancy Drew title, *Stay Tuned for Danger*. When the news came that the company was moving to Seattle, I'd had enough and gave my notice. However, that brought a different type of stress, as it left me in Albuquerque with no job and no job potentials. It took the help of friends and family, and the lucrative application of credit cards, to get back to Austin.

Gender-Inclusive Game Design

I would love to say *Gender Inclusive Game Design—Expanding the Market* was my idea, but honestly it wasn't. Charles River Media, a book publisher at the time, actually approached me with the idea of doing a book about making design choices that make games more approachable for women. They had seen me speak a number of times and believed what I was saying was important enough to become a book. I had some trepidation about it because I had never written a book before. The publisher was going through financial difficulties at the time and so I was left on my own to figure out the process ... which meant it nearly didn't get published at all! When it did finally come out in 2003, it received a nomination for Game Developer's Choice Book of the Year. Still today I am approached by women at game conferences who tell me my book influenced their choice to get into game development. Knowing that I've given women the courage to pursue their dreams is the single most important and most humbling thing I've done in my career.

Deciding to Stay

This was the final big decision point for me. It was 1997, I was back in Austin, but the game industry was not yet flourishing. It would have been the easiest and probably best thing for my health if I had stepped away. I admit, I thought long and hard about it. In the end, I decided my path was set. There was no choice for me but to follow my passion.

Over the next 18 years, I would start my own studio—twice, close it— twice, go to work for a game-tool developer, watch that get bought out and closed, write a book, go to work for a triple-A studio working on a movie-license game, watch that get run into the ground, build serious games, build educational games, work for at least one genius and work for a lot of not-so-geniuses. At the heart of it, there is one thing that has carried me through—the passion to design and build experiences that touch my players' emotions, to create experiences that take them away from their everyday lives to a place where they are the heroes. Every decision I have made, every road I have taken has always had that as the goal.

I won't say being a designer is easy. There will be bad experiences, doubts, heartache, and heartburn. But there will also be moments when a fan comes up and says, "Your game changed my life." That is why I make games. I wouldn't and couldn't have it any other way.

And yes, I still run a weekly paper-game group.

Endnotes

1. The *Ultima* series.
2. Boxed games came with registration cards that a player would fill out and send in after purchasing the game. This allowed us to have information on who was buying our games as well as give the player an easier way to get product support.
3. Computer Games Developers' Conference, later changed to simple GDC.

19

Write What You Know
How Female Writers Expand a Game's Audience

It shouldn't surprise anyone that people want characters they identify with. Think back to the 1990 release of Disney's *Beauty and the Beast*, and the generation of brunette little girls who were finally told you didn't have to be blonde to be beautiful. Even that single element of similarity (hair color) was enough to prompt loyalty from thousands of fans.

Games are no different. Yet, in 2012, the research firm EEDAR found that of 669 games with recognizable protagonists, only 24 were exclusively female.[1] Given that women represent 48% of game *players* and 50% of game *buyers*,[2] the dearth of playable characters leaves the industry at an obvious disadvantage. Eighty percent of game characters are also white,[3] making identification a problem for minorities as well as women.

Writers are often the difference between a game that relies on old tropes (We're looking at you, bald space marine …) and one that reaches for a broader audience. It is often the writer(s) on a game who decide characters' names and backgrounds. Even if writers don't get to decide which sneering badass to put on the box cover, they often do determine whether the world that badass lives in is made of 85% white men, or whether there is a more realistic balance of race and gender.

This isn't to say anyone should blame writers for the current representation problems. Writers are still few and far between at most game companies. For many games, a writer is hired for a brief contract after most development is done, to "pretty up" the words. But even those limited deals offer writers an opportunity. In a time when movie audiences still interpret a crowd with 17% women as being "half female," Geena Davis advises that writers can make a big difference just by going through a work and changing half the names to female.[4] In games, this can be as minor as reassigning a bunch of generic non-player characters (NPCs) to use a female body type and generic female bark file.

Becoming a Game Writer

There is still no single path to becoming a game writer. Some game writers come in with writing-specific degrees, but others have degrees in architecture, philosophy, or never completed college. Some companies believe only hiring a big-name screenwriter or novelist will suit their story. But some of the biggest developers still frequently hire writers with no published works, taking pride in the ability to recognize talent in a blind submission or piece of fanfic. If you're interested in breaking into game writing, cultivate the following:

- *Dialogue Writing:* Choose writing samples that show off dialogue, such as scripts or comic books, over prose writing like novels or blogs.
- *Modding:* Working on mods for games gives you experience with scripting and the challenges of implementing story in games.
- *GMing:* The experience of designing and running tabletop games is something game developers understand and gives you valuable experience understanding players.
- *Teamwork:* Any experience working on a team, taking and executing on feedback, is a useful thing to demonstrate, since a writer will never be the sole creator on a game.
- *Wide Range of Interests:* Having a broad base of knowledge is more important for game writers than schooling or technical knowledge.

Writing While Female

Writing seems to be one field in gaming in which women have reached parity, if not dominance, with some of the biggest names being women like Rhianna Pratchett of *Tomb Raider*. This means that as a female game writer, you may not face the "prove your cred" machismo that, say, female programmers can run into. However, this can also backfire. In a situation where writing is already considered a "soft" discipline of dubious importance, it can be doubly hard for female writers to be taken seriously.

And when you're the one who has to explain why having a quest revolve around saving the protagonist's raped and brutalized girlfriend might not be the most original or acceptable, it's easy for a writer to get dismissed as "oversensitive." The best thing to do in that situation is often to make it not about you. Bring the issue to other women in the company and find out how they react. Point to similar scenes in released games and any backlash that resulted. Even coming late to a project can be an advantage if you use it to remind the team that you approached this scene cold, as a player would, and this was your natural reaction.

Issues you are likely to face include:

- *Lack of Respect:* As a female writer, you may be talked down to, left out of key decisions and meetings that affect your work, or have your concerns dismissed. Be prepared to issue constant irritated reminders that you should be included in all meetings that involve character and story.
- *Technical Knowledge:* On the flip side, you may find programmers assuming that you have a more technical background and failing to explain basic functions in unfamiliar software. Be prepared to ask a lot of very clear basic questions.
- *Feedback Overload:* It's easier to criticize writing than code, so many people feel entitled to offer writing advice. Be prepared to separate yourself from your work and ruthlessly prioritize feedback so that you only use that which is frequent, relevant, fixable, and important.
- *Fans:* Fans have little idea what a writer does on a game, often assuming they have some kind of authorial control. Since many writers are active on social media (another place to put words!), they can be the first point of contact for abusive fans.

As a writer, you will be in the business of creating emotion. A well-written scene or character can plant a seed of change in someone's mind more effectively than a thousand angry screeds. So, get out there and write what you know. Your loves and hates and struggles will resonate with the struggles all players face. And by building that kind of empathy, your words can cross boundaries and maybe even change someone's life.

Endnotes

1. Kuchera, Ben. "Games with Exclusively Female Heroes Don't Sell (Because Publishers Don't Support Them)." *Penny Arcade Report.* 12 Nov 2012. Available at https://web.archive.org/web/20130321064024/http://www.penny-arcade.com/report/article/games-with-female-heroes-dont-sell-because-publishers-dont-support-them

2. Entertainment Software Association. "Essential Facts about the Computer and Videogame Industry." 2014. Available at http://www.theesa.com/wp-content/uploads/2014/10/ESA_EF_2014.pdf
3. Marks, Paul. "Videogames Need a More Diverse Cast of Characters." *New Scientist*. 22 Sept 2009. Available at http://www.newscientist.com/article/dn17819-video-games-need-a-more-diverse-cast-of-characters.html#.VaAx8_nYE75
4. Davis, Geena. "Geena Davis' Two Easy Steps to Make Hollywood Less Sexist (Guest Column)." *Hollywood Reporter*. 11 Dec 2013. Available at http://www.hollywoodreporter.com/news/geena-davis-two-easy-steps-664573

20

Megan Gaiser

Chief Executive Officer (CEO) and President: 1999–2013—Her Interactive, makers of the **Nancy Drew video game franchise**:

> *Nancy Drew: Secrets Can Kill, Nancy Drew: Stay Tuned for Danger, Nancy Drew: Message in a Haunted Mansion, Nancy Drew: Treasure in the Royal Tower*, and many more

Awards Received: Game Industry's "100 Most Influential Women," Next Generation 2010. "Top 10 Most Influential Women of the Decade," "IndieCade Honorary Trailblazer Award for Lifetime Achievement," IndieCade 2011. Gaming Angels 2009, "Microsoft Women in Games Award" 2010.

Creative Leadership for Human Sake

One day, with no warning, I *literally* went from Creative Director of a game company to CEO in an instant. I was sitting in a board meeting when the CEO stood up and resigned. The chairman of the board then looked at me and said, "We think you can do it." My reaction was visceral. I was sweating bullets. I became so pale that they took me into another room to give me some water.

I had no formal financial, management, or technical training. On paper, I was hardly the ideal candidate. I didn't think I was ready. But as it turned out, I had to be.

> *Say yes and you'll figure it out later.*
>
> **Tina Fey**

It was around the time game publishers deemed girls to be "ungameworthy" and refused to publish our first video game. The trouble with conventional wisdom is that it's often heavy on the conventional and light on the wisdom.

I was raised creatively, so I led that way. I had no clue how the game industry worked, so I sought out people who did. I cold-called CEOs. I found mentors for advice and support wherever I could. I hired people with different smarts and skills than I had. I hired business consultants who respected creativity. I could count the number of female CEOs in the game industry on one hand.

Our investors believed in the cause: *Video games designed for girls.* If we could demonstrate this was a lucrative value proposition, we would create an entirely new market niche. We had a vision: To inspire girls to lead through video games. At the time, it was new territory. Luckily, we didn't have to look far for inspiration. Nancy Drew, the heroine of the games we were making, never took no for an answer. And neither would we.

Nancy Drew embodies all the characteristics girls and women aspire to. She's smart, independent, bold, resourceful, and creative. We conducted one-on-one usability testing to understand what girls liked and disliked in existing games. Since there were no games for girls at the time, we had them play first-person shooters (FPS). They told us—"We don't mind shooting, but we'd prefer a reason. If they were after my little sister, I'd be all over them." So we added a mission statement at the start to give them some context.

We learned that the Nancy Drew character was perceived as being too perfect. The girls felt intimidated to role-play her. So we made her funny and a touch self-deprecating. They also thought it was lame to be required to start over following a fatal error. So we added a second chance button to replay the scene until they succeeded. It was no surprise that they also didn't appreciate being portrayed as sexual objects, victims or victims of violence. Being new at gaming, their fresh perspectives helped us to focus on improving existing gameplay rather than merely perpetuating gender stereotypes.

We blended entertainment and education throughout the narrative, environments, puzzles, and dialogue to expand the players' perspectives and world awareness. We integrated historical characters and cultural references to enhance the players' view of what was possible.

As a leader, I considered myself a part of the team. I viewed my role more as a collaborator and co-creator than an overseer and decider, although of course the buck stopped with me. We were a quirky, determined, and eclectic tribe. Respect for diversity of perspectives made it possible to collaborate across disciplines.

I let people know what I knew and what I didn't know. After all, no one could know (or pretend to know) everything. That would have ruined our flow. All ideas were welcome. The best ideas won.

This meant I had to embrace the unsettling feeling of chaos and uncertainty to create a space for new insights, original ideas, and progressive strategies. Being open to ambiguity and the unexpected created a space for diverse points of views because there were no preconceived notions, only possibilities.

The payoff was the courage to take more risks. That's how we transformed crisis into opportunities on a regular basis.

How to Build a Company by Serving an Imaginary Market (That Actually Exists)

I can speak confidently about our determination because it was tested early and often. We heard the usual "no's," but because we were talking to men about the inner lives of girls, we heard some unique and baffling "no's" as well. One reporter asked, "Why make games for girls?" Right, because ignoring half of your potential market is a winning strategy.

One publisher asserted as common knowledge that girls were computer-phobic; that technology, math, and females were a bad combination. Ada Lovelace was long gone and unavailable to provide the proof to the contrary, although I doubt it would have mattered. Our tagline we used at the time was, "For girls who aren't afraid of a mouse."

Another advised, "If you're going to make games for girls, make 'em pink and they'll come." We made them "unpink." They came and kept coming. We then changed our tagline to, "Dare to play."

Her Interactive Staff, Halloween 2003

We had presented the publishers with an amazing opportunity to create an entirely new market and revenue stream—but they were unable to see past their entrenched ways of doing business. As it turned out, there were a lot of females in the world! Their loss was our gain. We used our common (and uncommon) sense to carve a new path.

We had been refused retail entry through the front door, so we went in through the back. We ignored the naysayers, took a risk, and self-published with a tiny e-tail startup called Amazon. Game sales took off. The *New York Times* dubbed us the "UnBarbie" of computer games. Suddenly, the front door swung open.

We were like kids in a candy store, playing our way to success. People still told us we were crazy. But we were banking on being crazy wise.

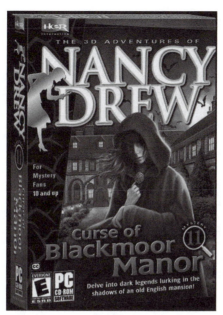

Nancy Drew: The Curse of
Blackmoor Manor, *Her Interactive
Office Party, 2004*

*Don't let the noise of others' opinions drown out your own inner voice. And
most important, have the courage to follow your heart and intuition.*

Steve Jobs

Creating and Enhancing Human and Financial Capital

We went from zero revenue to $8.5 million, sold over 9 million games, won 29 consecutive Parents' Choice awards and were the #1 PC adventure franchise in units, outselling *Harry Potter, Myst*, and *Lord of the Rings* for seven consecutive years. The *Nancy Drew* video game franchise became the predominant series for girls for many years.

We thought our target market for the *Nancy Drew* games would be girls aged 9 to 13. Initially, moms bought the games to inspire their daughters, just as they'd been inspired by the books as girls. And the girls did become hooked on the games, but so did the moms. So much so that the moms then gave the games to *their* mothers. Suddenly, we had a cross-generational phenomenon occurring, which led to our sales reaching demographics we never intended to hit.

Our games were fun and empowering—that's why they captured the imagination of so many girls, women, *and* boys. Over the years, fans of all ages sent thousands of testimonials to thank us. They described how the games motivated them to become scientists, NASA engineers, lawyers, detectives, cryptologists, and astronauts.

When girls came for tours, they met individually with the staff across disciplines to talk about their work and what it's like to create. When our fans left, they felt a foot taller, inspired to live out their future potential.

> *If she can see it she can be it.*
>
> **Geena Davis**

Our impact on these girls' lives fueled their confidence and that fueled our pride. Their testimonials gave us a reason to improve every day … with every game. We created a loyal and committed workforce who knew their ideas and contributions mattered not just in their jobs, but also in people's lives.

Reflecting on this, I now understand that our success resulted from our ability to design fun and meaningful engagement into every aspect of the company. Our shared vision led to a decade of inspired employees and players, award-winning products, yearly revenue growth, and for a long time, little competition.

Paying attention to female preferences not only made money, it broadened perspectives by flipping stereotypes on their heads. In the process, we created an entirely new market niche. We may have initially stumbled onto the art of creative collaboration, but after seeing the results, we continued to master it. We thrived in the game business for a decade.

The Crash, Fear, and Surrender

And then … the economy crashed and so did I. The game industry was hit hard. The combination of the economic downturn, revised business models, and platform changes required drastic and immediate measures to survive. I didn't have the appropriate senior-level executives in place to pivot the company. My efforts to find them proved to be too little, too late.

There are good times and bad times in business. I knew how to lead creatively in times of growth. Now I had to learn to apply those practices to a company in turmoil. Unfortunately, I gave in to fear, fear of change, fear of upsetting the status quo, fear of breaking old patterns, and ultimately, fear of losing what we had built. It knocked me off my feet.

I lost access to my curiosity, the gateway to creativity and the catalyst for courage. I then lost access to my best judgment and ultimately, my best self. I watched the collective intelligence dissipate. I now felt apart from, not a part of, the team.

Mistakes are the portal of discovery.

James Joyce

That was a wake-up call for me. I thought I'd mastered this ugly beast in the past, but there is nothing like a big, scary economy-tanking challenge to remind me that there's always more to learn.

As the CEO, I knew I was responsible. I had to make the painful decision to let some people go. Most had been with us for many years. I dreaded it. Then, I realized we could approach it the way we approached everything: differently.

We didn't take their keys, shut down their computers, and have security escort them out the door. We made a plan to support them through the entire process. We encouraged the rest of the company to do the same.

Instead of going into freeze-mode, everyone had a part to play. We told them how much they were valued. We helped them maintain their dignity. It kept us connected through our darkest hour. We found power in a seemingly powerless situation. Fortunately, the company survived. Rather than success, it was failure that made me a wiser leader and a better human being.

I left Her Interactive in 2013 after 15 years. I wondered how we were able to defy the odds in an environment where females were excluded. A few months passed. Suddenly, it hit me. The system didn't include us, so we forged our own path to redesign it. We succeeded because we went against the grain. We took risks to do what was necessary for a higher purpose.

Taking those risks enabled us to think and act differently. An unwelcoming environment provided us the opportunity to sidestep the status quo using creative collaboration.

I wondered if our experience had been an outlier—the exception, not the rule. If creative leadership was so effective, why was it so rare? Historically, creativity was often relegated to making art or products. I believe creative leadership has been underestimated because the value it brings couldn't be easily quantified.

What is creativity? The relationship between a human being and the mysteries of inspiration.

Elizabeth Gilbert

That's no longer the case. There is significant research and data underscoring both the logic and benefits of leading with creative intelligence. My experience echoed the research. The science of creativity has been proven. The value of creativity as a force for leadership that inspires the collective is undeniable. And the good news is it's teachable.

Creativity is a power within all of us. It's a way of being that uses all of our senses to empower us to sidestep what's not working, to make or do something better. A creative state of mind enables us to leverage both our acquired knowledge and innate wisdom to transcend traditional beliefs and established rules. It makes room for fresh perspectives.

Traditional leadership tends to value analytical intelligence (*logical, linear, and literal thinking*) as the primary driver, which may or may not include creative intelligence (*intuition, perception, sensing, feeling, imagination*). Creative leadership requires leading with creative intelligence supported by analytical intelligence. It fosters inclusivity and meaningful engagement.

This style of leadership focuses on what's possible for the greater good: for employees, for the products, and customers they serve. It encourages curiosity, kindness, courage, trust, risk-taking, resourcefulness, and playfulness.

It involves raising our awareness and, as a result, courage to lead in the moment, with an open mind (and open heart). Whether you call it conscious, creative, facilitative, or human-centered leadership, the basic tenets are the same.

Megan Gaiser and Nancy Drew Fans, 2001

The Tipping Point—Raising Consciousness for Humanity's Sake

The past few years have been a wake-up call for the game industry. Unconscious bias has been exposed as the root cause for a lack of diversity in our leadership and, as a result, a lack of diversity in our content. Both genders suffer from it; sexism, racism, and homophobia are a few of the results.

> *The truth we believe and cling to makes us unavailable to hear anything new.*
> **Pema Chodron**

As a result, the game industry continues to be predominantly shaped through the lens of one gender. And while it may be financially thriving, the culture remains uninspired. How can it be otherwise when we are still only accessing half of our collective intelligence to lead? Is this really the best we can do?

Hostility towards women still exists. There has been much controversy over the portrayal of women as sexual objects, victims, and victims of violence. Our girls had it right. The crux of the matter lies in the contention that all of our psyches—girls, women, boys and men—are being damaged by these portrayals of disrespect, violence, and anger. When we tell our sons that they are dominant and our daughters that they are unworthy, we rob both of the potential to become good leaders. And unless we stand up and object to this message, we are saying it is okay.

Unconscious bias is a bad habit, a blind spot we all have. It prevents us from welcoming diverse people and perspectives. Because it's unconscious, we often don't realize it exists within us. What's worse, we often think we're immune, and therefore, impartial. It's an unconscious *bias* ... so we think we're right.

How do we combat unconscious bias? Perhaps the answer is to challenge those belief systems. If we can recondition how we think, and reshape our beliefs, we can positively transform our behavior and the output of teams. Embracing techniques to observe our thoughts, judgments and emotions instead of being ruled by them, feeds our connection with instead of bias towards, each other.

Leadership creates culture. Culture creates consciousness. And our consciousness creates the media products we interact with. Since the quality of our leaders determines the quality of everything, unconscious bias is the enemy of inclusivity, diversity, and inspired innovation.

Becoming a real human being is the primary leadership issue of our time,
but on a scale never required before.

Betty Sue Flowers

Making Meaning and Money

We need the best creative minds at all levels of our industry. People need to be inspired, not merely managed. Inspiration that speaks to our deepest values offers us a higher purpose for what we do. We upgrade our computers when they no longer function at their maximum capacity. Why wouldn't we upgrade ourselves to function at our maximum human capacity?

Creativity is the most important skill in the 21st century and the most valuable leadership tool we can employ. By tapping into something larger than ourselves, creative leadership fosters commerce in the interests of the greater good. Some call this flow. Some call this love. Some call this source. I call it creativity.

Imagine a future where women and men feel safe to bring their entire selves to work to truly collaborate for inspired innovation. Imagine business models that serve the interests of shareholders, boards, employees, and customers. Imagine discovering new economic arenas by intuiting market opportunities. Imagine the still undreamt original products, new market niches, and revenue streams waiting to be created.

Imagine games that respect rather than denigrate human life, that fill us up rather than dumb us down. Imagine being enriched rather than being manipulated by media. Imagine developing multisensory games using our innate wisdom as the language to drive the underlying code. Imagine shaping the emergent mediums of virtual and augmented reality through the lens of both genders. Imagine unleashing our full human potential.

Don't think about making women fit the world. Think about making the
world fit women.

Gloria Steinem

Creativity is our human operating system. It accesses all domains of knowing. It knows no bounds of culture, creed, gender, or race. Just think what we could achieve together if we said "no" to fear and "yes" to creativity to discover the transformative possibilities before us. Imagine what we could achieve if we weren't afraid.

21

Kari Toyama

Steam Hardware Team: *SteamVR, HTC Vive, Steam Controller, Steam Link*

Producer: *Project Wayward* (canceled)

Producer/Quality Assurance (QA) Project Manager: *Peggle 2*

QA: *Gears of War: Judgment, Age of Empires Online, Lips, Lost Odyssey, Halo 3*

The first video game I remember playing was *Mike Tyson's Punch Out!* at my babysitter's house. She had a grandson who was 10 years older than me. His arm was amputated when he was younger and he played against me holding the controller with one hand. I did not win a single game, but I didn't want to stop playing. It was the beginning of a long love affair with games.

Growing Up Nerd

My mother is a nerd. We always had at least two PCs in the house, and she ran a MUD (multi-user dungeon) with our stepfather. My first PC games were *Duke Nukem*, *DOOM*, and *Myst* (my favorite, although I was too young to really be able to crack those puzzles). We were allowed to have one console in the house, always donating the previous one when we upgraded. My brother and I grew up with the NES[1], SNES[2], Sega Genesis, Sega Dreamcast, Nintendo 64, and PlayStation 2. We took turns playing (except for those rare times when we found a great co-op game) and had to play in the living room rather than tucked away in our own bedrooms. This was our parents' way of being a part of our gaming and it worked out well for us. Even when my brother started playing *Asheron's Call* for ungodly numbers of hours, it was always in the living room where the rest of the family was.

It didn't occur to me when I was younger that I could have a career in video games. Still, I was naturally drawn to careers that weren't really considered normal for women. My top two favorites were archeologist (Indiana Jones) and FBI agent (Mulder and Scully). I always wanted to be one of the boys, striving to do anything they could do. I learned to drive stick-shift, ride a motorcycle, and open a beer bottle with my teeth—basically anything that would get them to take me seriously.

Secret Dancer

I danced ballet in an after-school program for seven years. Since I was such a tomboy, I didn't want my male classmates to know. I wanted them to think I only played basketball. Once I was getting ready for our annual recital to start, with the tiara and fancy makeup, and a group of boys had just finished basketball practice when they spotted me. They were in complete shock and I remember one of them saying, "Kari? Uh ... You're in ... Ballet?" Busted!

I was studying psychology in college and working the graveyard shift at a 24-hour grocery store when I became part of an all-female *Halo 2* clan called The Cavegirls. We were very active in the *Halo* community and eventually befriended a few employees at Bungie. After playing over 5,000 multiplayer sessions in *Halo 2*, and with the help of some of my new Bungie friends, I applied for an entry-level contract tester role on *Halo 3*. They took a chance on me because I was a referral and I had to be interviewed twice in person because I was such a noob and there were no women on the test team at the time. To my surprise, they hired me, and I took a 50% pay cut to work with the coolest people on Earth.

Breaking In: The Dream Career

I remember being very nervous my first day at Bungie. I was hired as a BVT (build verification test) tester and my team's job was to verify that the build that had been cooking the night before was working well enough for the rest of the studio to use for development. We were the first people to arrive at work; our shift was 6:30 a.m. to 2:30 p.m. The team was about 20 people and I was the only woman. Before my start date, the lead had told the rest of the team that I was some sort of tournament-level *Halo* player and therefore really good at the game. I had participated in one tournament and was decent at *Halo*, but definitely nowhere near a professional level. At the end of my first week, we played a free-for-all match on the latest *Halo 3* build. I was really nervous to play with my team on a competitive level for the first time, so I just gave it everything I had, and I absolutely crushed them. I was so nervous, my hands were shaking, and the only thing I could say was, "Good game, boys."

Since most of us were entry-level testers, being on the BVT team meant there was an opportunity to move to another team with more responsibilities. I worked as hard as I could so that I would stand out and get promoted, and it worked. I was asked to join a small team of three people and was given area-ownership for the first time (I owned the saved films feature). I wrote my first test pass and got the chance to work with some of the most talented people at Bungie.

After *Halo 3* shipped, the majority of the test team was reassigned to other Microsoft Game Studios projects. I was reassigned to *Lost Odyssey*, and that ended my stint at Bungie. I was pretty bummed that I wouldn't be working at my favorite game studio, but determined to keep advancing my new career path.

Moving Forward

I spent the next five years as a contract tester working on multiple AAA titles with great people at Microsoft. But it's difficult to stand out in a room filled with dozens of other testers. As I continued to hone my testing skills, I yearned for more responsibility and recognition.

Being a contractor at Microsoft has its ups and downs, although most testers would probably say the negatives outweigh the positives. I was thankful that someone even considered hiring me in the first place, so I approached contracting in a positive way. Contractors don't have as much responsibility as full-time staff, which meant I could focus on the projects and tasks in front of me and not worry about accountability or company impact. That doesn't mean I didn't care about my team or company; it just meant I didn't have to worry how my manager would grade me during an annual review (because there were no reviews for contractors). We also billed for overtime, and that was really nice during all those crunch hours. This has since changed at Microsoft, but contract testers took a mandatory 90-day unpaid break after (a maximum of) 12 months of work. The upside to this policy was that I could travel during my breaks. My partner and I had wonderful experiences in places like Italy, New Zealand, and Hawaii, but because of the long breaks, I never felt like I was truly a part of the team that I loved to work with year after year.

The First Crunch

One week during *Halo 3* development, there was an issue with our live multiplayer beta and they asked people to stay to test a hotfix as soon as possible. I logged so many hours that week that I was asked to double check the numbers. Apparently I set a record. It was the first time I experienced a team push like that, and it was incredibly exciting. The next person to beat my record was my own brother, a year later.

In my six years at Microsoft, I was promoted five times. Three of those promotions happened because I asked for them. I remember wanting to work on the core test team which was located in another building at Microsoft. My team mostly corresponded with them via intercompany chat and every once in a while they'd come to our building and meet with us in person, which meant we didn't have a normal face-to-face relationship. I had already reached the highest level in my group and the core team was the only way to move forward. I knew the only way to get them to consider bringing me over was to ask them, so I did. The day before my 90-day break I asked the team lead if I could meet with him at his office and told him I was interested in working directly on his team. He said he would bring me on and marked my return date on his calendar. He made good on his word. And I learned to follow my gut.

Being a part of the core test team meant that I could own more areas and work directly with the publishing team. In 2012, I was promoted to the highest level of contract tester at Microsoft and joined the *Gears of War: Judgment* team. After contracting with Microsoft for several years and hitting the level ceiling, I had been working toward getting a full-time position on the test team. Working closely with the test lead, Jim Griffin, I went above and beyond what was expected of me during that year on *Gears*. He was an excellent manager and always encouraged me when I wanted to improve our processes. Yet even with the great mentorship and guidance I had from my team, and my passion for the projects, I was still never even considered for a permanent position.

Peggle 2

Determined to take my career into my own hands, I reached out to a long-time industry friend, Allen Murray. Allen and I met playing *Halo 2* before I started working in games. He was at Bungie for several years and eventually made his way to PopCap Games. I was a huge fan of PopCap, so I messaged Allen about possible opportunities there. On his referral, I interviewed for a full-time test lead position on one of their mobile titles, but the team didn't feel like I had the mobile experience. But the test director, Michael Cook, saw something in me and asked me to come in for another interview with the *Peggle* team. They had just made a deal with Microsoft that would make *Peggle 2* a timed-exclusive launch-window title for their next-gen console, the Xbox One. I met with the team and they made an offer before I even left the studio.

Working on *Peggle 2* was the highlight of my career so far. When I started, the team was unsure how I would handle a small team after working in a very corporate environment for so long. I had a lot to prove. I really wanted the team to trust me and I wanted to help them make the best game packed with rainbow farts, unicorns, and *Ode to Joy* blaring from our speakers.

The *Peggle* team had a long history before I arrived and they were suffering from low morale and high turnover. As the test lead, I was part of the leadership team, which included the producer, art director, lead designer, audio lead, and engineering lead. Together, we made all the decisions that would affect the project (a first for me). There were a lot of firsts for me during the project. I became a hiring manager, I put together my own test team, I served as the point of contact for EA's localization and certification teams, I maintained a positive and successful relationship with our remote test teams, and I successfully shipped my first game as a test lead (on time, and on a brand new console!). More importantly, I helped bring the team together and got them excited about shipping a great product.

After we launched *Peggle 2*, the team had plans to work on downloadable content (DLC) and bring the game over to other consoles. Unfortunately, we lost our fantastic producer and fearless leader, Jared Neuss, a couple months after the initial launch. To my surprise, PopCap asked if I'd be interested in taking over for Jared. I had no clue they were even considering me for the job because I didn't think I was qualified. I remember Jared saying, "Kari, you know what it takes to run this team. You'd be great at it." I took some time to think about whether I wanted to move out of test as I was doing very well as a test lead and really enjoyed being part of the improvement and growth of the QA department there. Ultimately, I decided to move into production because it was a new challenge.

After a series of ridiculous events, I found out that there was no headcount available in the production department, so they couldn't offer me the title. *Peggle 2* still needed a producer and I agreed to temporarily run the project while they found a replacement from another project. I figured I would be in the position for two or three weeks and I could learn some things while I was at it. I ended up running *Peggle 2* as both the producer and test lead for eight months. In that time, I was also promoted to QA Project Manager, which meant more management responsibility within PopCap and EA Mobile. My vision for sustaining *Peggle 2* was to address the top requests from the community, deliver a few pieces of really fun DLC, and launch on another console. We eventually shipped six DLC updates, launched on PlayStation 4 (another first for me), and successfully integrated features based on feedback from our players.

I learned to build a trusting relationship with my team by being empathetic to their needs and their work. I learned that if my team trusts me, they'll rally behind me, and together we'll inspire others and make incredible games. I learned to be more confident in myself and my work because I am very good at what I do.

Conclusion

I hope that a young woman is reading this book right now. And even if that young woman isn't interested in games or game testing or production, she'll probably go through the same types of struggles I've had in her career and life. I want that young woman to know that once I figured out what I wanted to do with my life, nothing was going to stop me. It took me six years to get to where I really wanted to be, and it was worth it because I gained immeasurable skills from my experiences along the way.

My advice to young women is to work hard, always do more than is expected of you, never stop learning, find mentors that inspire you (and learn from their mistakes as well as their successes), get respect by giving respect, surround yourself with positive people in both professional and personal spaces, always follow up with people and keep in touch with anyone you respect, don't let hateful comments get in your way, and never be afraid to follow your gut.

Endnotes

1. Nintendo Entertainment System.
2. Super Nintendo Entertainment System.

22

Good, Fast, or Cheap
What Does a Game Producer Do, Anyway?

If you're wondering what exactly a producer does, you're not the only one. Even within the industry, there is debate as to whether producers are necessary, with some indie studios foregoing the role to "keep more control in the hands of the creators," while in other companies producer titles proliferate to the point of resentment from the programmers, artists, and designers who see themselves as the "real" developers.

In Hollywood, there's a joke: "How do you become a producer? Get a desk." This refers to the fact that "producer" credits are far less regulated than other roles in film production and are frequently handed out as rewards to people with tangential roles in making the film. The situation isn't as bad in gaming, but there is still great confusion over what exactly a producer does to make a game. This is partly because producers can have a wide variety of job titles and responsibilities at different companies, from "project managers" who are the buck-stops-here leaders of their game team, to "product managers" who coordinate budgets and schedules, to junior producers whose responsibilities vary depending on who needs what done that day.

For our purposes, production is the discipline that deals with the nuts and bolts of shipping a game: How many programmers do we need to hire to have a game engine up and running by our March 16 deadline? How much will that cost? Producers make the schedules and crunch the budgets and make sure other departments aren't running over ... or if they are, it's for a good enough reason to revise those master documents yet again. Producers are the people at your company who can never forget the conundrum that you can't make a game good *and* fast *and* cheap; you can only pick two of the three.

To make those decisions, producers must be organized, big-picture thinkers, *and* possess the people skills to communicate with every developer. Often, producers act as the go-between to help different departments communicate. When marketing needs a new trailer put together by artists and writers who have already been crunching for two months on a new feature, it is a producer who talks to both sides to learn what marketing really needs (not wants) and what the developers have the time and ability to do.

Production also tends to be one of the more female-driven departments in a lot of game studios, with "producers" and "business and management" both reporting 21% to 22% female staffs in Gamasutra's annual survey, compared to 5% of programmers and 9% of artists.[1] These ratios both contribute to and suffer from the stereotype that women aren't "real developers." So, just to nip that notion in the bud—producers may not create the code or assets that go into a game, but they are a core part of development teams. In addition to the rest of their work, they often serve as early quality assurance on a project, regularly playing the game while it's in development to offer crucial feedback on bugs, functionality, and fun in early stage projects. On live games, producers are the ones working weekends to make sure that Monday morning's content drop goes smoothly for players.

Becoming a Producer

To become a producer, you should be an organized self-starter: many of your weekly deliverables will be things like deliverable breakdowns for 50 other team members and budgets in the tens of millions of dollars. You need enough technical background to talk to a team of programmers about mysqladmin errors, and enough communication skills to come back to a team of artists and explain what that means. In games with microtransactions or player metrics collected by the game, it is often a producer sorting the data of what sold well or which features kept new players engaged.

Much game development uses the Agile development process, in which "teams respond to unpredictability through incremental, iterative work cadences,"[2] meaning development teams are divided into small groups who work on short-term goals (sprints), and reevaluate those goals frequently (every two to three weeks), so no one ever goes off-track for long. There are various live and online courses to allow aspiring producers to become Certified ScrumMasters, the team leaders of Agile development.[3]

Basic project management software such as Project Manager, JIRA, Trello, or Asana are also an essential part of a producer's arsenal. A good producer will know every trick Excel can do and some even Microsoft never noticed.

Forming a Studio

More and more frequently, people don't wait to get jobs in the industry, opting instead to form their own studios and just get their game out to the public. In the indie world, almost all game developers are producers, whether they like it or not. When a programmer or designer starts her own studio, she often must take a crash course in production skills, learning how to estimate budgets and time-lines and how to manage freelancers or employees from different specialties and backgrounds. Whatever the title of an indie studio founder, you can bet that many of her day-to-day responsibilities fall under the rubric of "production."

If you go this route, try to learn as much as you can about game development first, so you don't have to reinvent the wheel. It's all too common at GDC to see a mid-sized studio talk about their growing pains as they went from a bunch of guys in their pajamas to a studio with Scrum teams, formal development processes, and a human resources department. "We realized that our games come out on time more often when we set a budget and cut features," they proclaim triumphantly, year after year, as if they are the first to have ever had this revelation.

To avoid this, build awareness of good production practices into your very first game. Even if you're doing all of the art, design, and programming yourself, set a deadline you want to hit and a price point at which your game can make a profit. Unless you know how many (wo)man-hours of actual work it took to get that first game out the door, you won't know how many programmers or artists to hire now that you're successful enough to expand!

Endnotes

1. "Gamasutra's Annual Game Developer's Salary Survey." 2015. Pages 2–3. Available at http://www.gamesetwatch.com/2014/09/05/GAMA14_ACG_SalarySurvey_F.pdf
2. "What is Agile,?" Agile Methodology. 23 Oct 2008. Available at http://agilemethodology.org/
3. "Certifications in Scrum, the Leading Framework for Agile Software Development." Scrum Alliance. Available at https://www.scrumalliance.org/certifications

23

Katie Postma

Community Manager: *Uru: Ages Beyond Myst, Uru: Path of the Shell, Uru: To D'ni, Prince of Persia: Warrior Within, Myst IV: Revelation, Myst V: End of Ages, FusionFall, Dance Mela, Stargate Worlds, Mass Illusions, Jumpgate Evolution, Battle Punks, Fish World, Game of Thrones Ascent, Star Trek Timelines*

Like so many of the extraordinary women in this book, I fell into the world of game development by happy accident.

My husband and I were newly married in 1995, and friends of ours had a brand new PC. They purchased several games, one of which was *Myst*. We spent many evenings together with a small group of friends pouring over the island and its puzzles. When we got stuck, I went into a chatroom for *Myst* fans (Cyan Chat) and found many players happy to help us around our hurdles. But something else happened the moment I logged in … I felt like

I had found "my people." People from around the world who liked to share their own game experiences with each other? I was hooked.

Several years and two children later, we bought our own PC and *Myst* and *Riven* were the first games we purchased. Again, when I was stuck I sought out Cyan Chat and my fellow *Myst* fans (now friends) to help me out. I was a stay-at-home mother by this point, and because my children were small and napped frequently, I began to go into the chatroom on a daily basis to help others as I had been helped, which seemed only fair!

Over time, some players came to consider me a volunteer leader and gave me a moderation spot on the forums at mystcommunity.com. I created a persona and did everything I could to make sure all *Myst* fans had a rich and rewarding community experience. Of course, at the time, I felt like all I was doing was being helpful, friendly, and giving back to the community who had already given me so much.

Going Pro

The next year, Ubisoft called and asked me to interview for their Community Manager position for the *Myst* franchise. I was stunned, and honored. My husband and I determined this would be a tremendous opportunity for me, and thus I began a career which has lasted more than 15 years. I've worked for many game companies which make massively multiplayer online role-playing games (MMORPGs), social and mobile games, and even some social apps outside the game industry. But I always felt that connection to my first "community"—the *Myst* players.

The fans themselves taught me a great deal about what it means to manage a community. One time, when I was new on the job, I was happily posting through what is politely referred to in the biz as a "shitstorm." I figured if I pushed my way and my viewpoint hard enough, players would fall into line. They did not. Three of my most prolific (and brilliant) community members firmly and respectfully put me in my place. They then proceeded to antagonize each other and everyone around them for pages and pages of a forum thread one could only deem "epic." After a few days and a few sleepless nights, I asked all three gentlemen to join me on a Skype voice call. I asked them all, in turn and with each of the others listening, to explain why and how they felt their own ideas were good ones. What followed was one of my greatest memories and achievements as a community manager: all three agreed they were there for the same reasons—to have fun, to help others, and to make the game great. I deputized all of them to join our team of volunteer moderators and that team ended up seeing me through many rough moments, including the cancelation of *Uru* and my decision to leave Ubisoft.

Prior to the call from Ubisoft, I was a stay-at-home mother of two for seven years. Before I had children, I had worked as an office administrator in many different industries such as banks, colleges, hospitals, and law firms. Prior to that, I had waitressed before college, and I babysat as a teenager. The service industry and babysitting roles probably prepared me more than anything for a job in community management. The desire to keep people happy and satisfied, as well as a great deal of patience and understanding, is key to surviving players' unhappy moments. I've heard community managers described as "eating bees," "ministers of culture," "babysitters," and "police." Somewhere between all those is where a good community manager finds herself: caring, honest, and willing to make the needs of others her priority.

With each day and each title, I strive to make all players feel that sense of community I first felt with *Myst*. Every player has their own experience and story, something that brings them into the game and keeps them coming back. If I can explore that and get them to share their passion with others, connections are made and the community becomes a rich, rewarding, and vibrant place to be online.

Moving On

After working with the *Myst* community for Ubisoft for two years, I was offered a job at a start-up for a new MMORPG in development, *Stargate Worlds*. Three years and millions of dollars later, that game was canceled and I was frustrated, sad, and scared for the future of my career and games in general. It wasn't just about the fact that thousands of hours of programming, art, and writing had been wasted, but that the fledgling community I had facilitated—"my" new community of potential players—had been so carelessly let down. It was hard to know that all the passion and support I had nurtured in the community had been squandered on a game no one would ever get to play.

I kept in touch with many of those players and volunteers. I still chat with some of them to this day, 12 years later. Building a community is about so much more than just a game or a studio; it makes it difficult to "move on." That's because a good community's raison d'être is always to keep people together.

Over time I was extremely fortunate to work with many large studios on some terrific titles such as Cartoon Network for *FusionFall*, Gazillion for *Jumpgate Evolution*, and Big Viking Games for *Fish World*. Nothing got me as excited as working with the players, fans, and supporters of these games and nothing was ever as rewarding as making these supporters happy. Today I work at another start-up—Disruptor Beam—on two tremendous franchises (*Game of Thrones* and *Star Trek*), and after three and a half years, I can safely and thankfully say this team supports community like no other I've been with. Our CEO is a huge proponent of community as the backbone of any game and I've always had the full support of the team to make things "right" for our players. It's a terrific feeling to be somewhere that recognizes and values the players as vital to the health of any game or development team.

What Makes a Great Community

Throughout the years I've learned a few things about what makes a truly great community; one that will welcome and keep its players for years and years:

- *Honesty without Burden*: Let your player base know what's going on with development, without giving them so much information that they are robbed of their joy of the game. Tell them if something is broken, even tell them why, without giving so many technical details you bore them or cause them more concern than needed.
- *Kindness without Expectation*: Be generous and give to your players without expecting anything in return. Do not give them a "sale" hoping to get their return business; do it because you appreciate them. Without them you wouldn't be here, so never take them for granted.
- *Recognize and Appreciate the Big Picture*: When messaging or responding to your players, make sure you remember that they're all there to have fun and play together. Try not to get bogged down in the minor details or react to unimportant differences of opinion. And never, ever post while angry.

Those three principles can keep a community running smoothly for years and years, without being derailed by any small bumps. As well, it's important to invest in the natural leaders in your community; find the people who have a strong influence, who share your core values, and then "harness their powers for good," as I like to call it. Having devoted fan leaders and cheerleaders is a crucial part of keeping your community going.

It's imperative if you're working in a community role to make sure you surround yourself with positive people, and ask for help if you need it. It's also important that you take breaks when you need them, make sure you're being proactive and not reactive, and never respond to a player or team member when you're upset. Take a walk or take a time out to remember that often what's being said is not personal; a player who is frustrated or having a bad day may say or do something they would not otherwise do. It's essential to let that player know that, while their bad behavior won't be tolerated, we value them as a player and a human being.

I have had the good fortune to meet and recruit dozens of tremendous, passionate, compassionate fans, who saw what my communities needed and helped me forge a great foundation of new players, resurrect a disheartened group of players, or even turn around some disenfranchised players. The key isn't to build an army of corporate spokespeople, but to surround yourself with well-intentioned people who want the best for the community (not always the same thing as the game or the company!) and are willing to put their time toward that goal. And remember, they may have very differing opinions on how to go about achieving that goal. In fact, the more varied personalities and playstyles you have in your core group of community advocates, the better it is for the community as a whole. What you believe is best may not always be, and working with those who can see things differently can let you reach a happy compromise.

As I learned on *Myst*, I'm only as good as the people who alert me to problems, identify issues, and support the community with me. In fact, without those volunteers and part-time contractors, I probably would not have stayed in the field or had as much success as I have. Any time I can, I try to reward these volunteers and helpers with something special so they feel valued and understand how much they do for me and the community—real-life swag, in-game rewards, or even direct access to myself and the development team. Rewarding loyalty motivates and encourages the best people to do their best work, which in turn reflects well on me and the company.

Being Human

The most relevant part of a community manager's job is emotional—honesty, kindness, loyalty—these are what make a game community transcend the game worlds we're playing in. We're sharing an experience far beyond our in-game "XP." We're being human together. The game or the community channels based on that game are just a backdrop for a larger gathering of like-minded folks. I've met many, many players "IRL" and if you take the game away, I'd still like to meet them, chat, or have a beer with them. And like anyone you meet, you feel their loss keenly. Some players wander off or vanish, some are taken quite suddenly through illness or death. These are the moments when you realize your "job" has bled over into the rest of your life, when you miss these people deeply and for years.

In my current role at Disruptor Beam, I have met thousands of people who care deeply about our game and each other. Some of our players have received great joy from playing *Game of Thrones Ascent* because it takes them out of their real world and puts them in a world where they can be a noble of Westeros, free from pain, or disability, or other burdens in their real lives. In a couple of cases, we've been able to put unique items or content into the game as tributes to players who have died or are fighting terrible illnesses, and to memorialize their amazing strength and spirit. Some may have never realized how much they brightened my days and the lives of the community members around them. Some, I had the opportunity to tell in time. All will be remembered for how awesome they were.

One player, Sue (known in-game as "the Countessa") underwent surgery but then unexpectedly passed away. We were informed by her fellow guild members that her daughter was receiving support, both emotional and financial, from Sue's in-game friends. When we heard she had died, we were quite upset and many of our team felt we should do something. We worked with our design team and producer to create special quests and an item for her, The Countessa's Handkerchief, to express our sorrow.

As a community manager, I never have to doubt whether my work is pure entertainment, or whether that entertainment has real-world value. In hearing from real players how our games impact their lives—even just by letting them escape from them—I know that we're doing something important.

In memory of Pepsi, Aquila, and the Countessa.

24

Donna Prior

Community Manager Team Lead: *TERA*

Community Representative: *Star Wars: The Old Republic*

Community Moderator: *Pirates of the Burning Sea*

Community Manager: *Gods & Heroes: Rome Rising, Planetside 2, Bullet Run*

Community Coordinator: *Guild Wars II*

Co-Founder: IGDA Community Management Special Interest Group

The Sparkly Princess of Social Media and Community Management

Okay, so maybe I'm not that sparkly. And certainly not a princess. At least, I wasn't growing up. I read everything I could get my hands on. I was a lonely, quiet, and painfully shy child. My report card from first grade touched on this: my teacher wrote, "Donna needs to learn to socialize with other children. She spends every recess under a tree reading."

As I got older, I did manage to make friends. I have two younger brothers, and it always seemed like my neighborhood had lots of boys. Unsurprisingly, as I got older, my hobbies were all "boys' things." And the one thing I wanted to do the most was play *Dungeons & Dragons*.

In Texas, back in the late 1970s/early 1980s, gender rules were pretty structured. I never gave it much thought until my friends told me, "Girls don't play D&D." I was pretty angry, but figured I was the defective one and they were right. I tried to get into more "girly" things, but it didn't work.

I continued to escape into stories, and sunk my life into working, partying, and … roller skating.

Ironically, while bartending in San Antonio, I met some awesome people who invited me to play D&D with them. Out of my mouth came those old words, "But girls don't play D&D." How wrong I was! This group had two other women in it already. They invited me in, and Aubrey Bloodmane, Ranger & follower of Sune, was created. I had found my home in Faerûn.

Getting Technical

Eventually, I moved to Austin. My friends and family started telling me that I should get a "real job," settle down, and start a family. I ended up applying for a customer service position in the now-defunct Dell Factory Outlet. I knew nothing about computers, but somehow I got the job. I spent the next 14 years in tech support, doing hardware and software support. Mostly, I liked what I did, but had a lot of difficulty managing corporate politics. One of the things which made life more bearable was my old D&D group getting together monthly to play *Magic: The Gathering*. We were terrible, but we didn't care. We loved it.

"Girls Don't Play Games. Girls Don't Like Tech. Girls Are Bad at It. Why Don't You Like Being Called a Girl?"

This litany has been such a refrain in my life that it has been impossible not to internalize it. In 2006, I was shocked when I found myself telling a Privateer Press employee, who wanted to give me a *Warmachine* demo, "Women don't play miniatures games." That moment made me realize I had to fight those stereotypes, and this has guided me for the past eight years in the game industry. Girls and women *do* play games. We *make* games. We *are* games. And we're not going away.

Shall We Play a Game?

All this time, I continued to sporadically play tabletop RPGs. It was always hard to find a group that would welcome new players, and the ones that did were often terrible.

I also picked up my very first video game, *The Sims*. I joined a lot of communities around *The Sims* and its user-generated content. Some of the friends I met through these communities started talking about a beta test for an online version, called *The Sims Online*. I signed up immediately.

It truly was a brand new world. I promptly ran into actual people I knew "In Real Life." I realized that on the other side of every avatar was a real person. We formed bonds across the world, sharing our ups and downs with our beloved beta community. Then some players told me, "Hey, you're a big *Star Wars* fan, right? You should apply for the beta for *Star Wars Galaxies*." And I did.

Star Wars Galaxies. I don't think I have enough room in this chapter to explain what this game meant to me. As they say, it was the best of times, it was the worst of times. But when interacting with the community and moderators for the game, I got my first inkling that what I loved doing had a title and could be a career.

Breaking In

In the 14 years I was in information technology (IT), I had been a contractor, moving around quite a bit. But now, my mother was ill and I wanted to move home to Seattle. Outside of work, I continued to spend my time going to Renaissance Festivals, playing video games, attending conventions, and spending hours each day on game forums.

In 2006, I found *Pirates of the Burning Sea*, by Flying Lab Software. As someone who loves tall ships and the Age of Sail, I fell in love with the company and the community. I went to PAX in 2006 to meet the developers and hang out at the big fan party. As soon as I got to the Flying Lab booth, I immediately jumped in and started helping. I was there with a clipboard, signing folks up for the beta. I was assisting Community Director Troy Hewitt by handing out t-shirts and swag. I had an amazing time helping; it's what I love to do. I got so involved that some of the FLS team thought I was a new hire.

Eventually, my involvement with the FLS community consumed my other hobbies. Troy offered me a full-time job, and I took a pay cut to become a community moderator in 2007. It was worth every penny I didn't earn to learn about the industry and my new career path as a community manager.

Two years later, I took another contract gig with BioWare, as a community representative on *Star Wars: The Old Republic*. It was tremendously exciting: Sean Dahlberg believed in me, even without knowing me in person. I loved being on a team of people who really understood the value of community, while being super fans of everything *Star Wars*. This wasn't just another gig in games; this was *STAR WARS*. This team was the only one I couldn't beat in *Star Wars* trivia. Many had worked on *Star Wars Galaxies*, and loved the *Star Wars* Expanded Universe. This wasn't lip service to fandom. From the executive-level doctors,[1] down to QA and community, everyone was a *Star Wars* fan. We understood what this game meant to each other and to our players. That job brought my life full circle; from fan on *Star Wars Galaxies* to *professional* fan and community representative on *SWTOR*.

After my contract ended, I moved to Austin, to work for Heatwave Interactive as the community manager for *Gods & Heroes: Rome Rising*. The dev team there was a bunch of cantankerous grognards, but they respected me, and took a chance on all the outrageous community-driven schemes I threw at them, even emerging from their caves to participate in live streams and other social events. (I'm telling you, it's amazing what promises of pizza and beer can do!) I still keep in touch with a lot of people from this tiny community. They were incredibly engaged; many of them came from the old *Gods & Heroes* community (from when Perpetual Entertainment owned it). And, as always, it was a great learning experience for my next gig.

Always the Next Gig

Alas, in the game industry, there is always a next gig. As *Gods & Heroes* slowly started shutting down, I looked elsewhere. I had always wanted to work with Linda Carlson, so it was easy for me to say yes to taking a social media specialist gig at Sony Online Entertainment in San Diego.

Unfortunately, sometimes you aren't a good fit for a company. And sometimes they're a terrible fit for you. I was very grateful for the opportunity, but I think everyone was relieved (including myself) when I was laid off after my game shut down.

Even in a job I knew wasn't working out, there were a lot of good things that happened: I enjoyed working cross team with legal and security; I learned a lot about social media, taught the community team things they didn't know, and helped fine tune the streaming. I worked with some super smart people and even took on my own wee community for *Bullet Run*. Yes, I know you've never heard of it either. But I loved my little community and was sad to see the game be shut down.

I got to interact with the *Star Wars Galaxies* community. I was there when the game logged off, playing with my original guildmates and friends. I still cry thinking about it.

Such is life as a game industry CM.

The siren call of Seattle was loud in my head, so I moved back. A few months later, one of my favorite people, Martin Kerstein of ArenaNet, asked if I was free to work. I'm a huge fan of *Guild Wars 2*, so I jumped at the chance to work on the community team as a community coordinator.

The *Guild Wars 2* community is amazing. I was so blessed to work with a great team. I did some of my favorite work, from revamping internal processes, to facilitating conversation between players and developers. I love that many *Guild Wars 2* players still keep in touch and invite me to play with them.

That's one of the things community managers do. We put a real face on development. The players feel more invested and they trust us, and by extension trust the company. I met an incredible number of people who recognized my main character's name when they met me in-game. I'd run "flagged" as ArenaNet Staff, and I would run into people who said "I remember when you were on the Community Team for _____ game. I really felt you listened and we had such a good time. Thank you!"

That's what community management is about—building relationships, forging bonds, making sure the players are having a good time, and if not, listening to them and understanding how to make it better.

Community Management in the Game Industry

Here's the thing about community management. People don't always under-stand what we do. People in the industry and out. Community managers act as advocates for the players, and do their best to bridge communication between players and development teams. Unfortunately, we're often quite terrible at getting our voices heard! Good CMs are empathetic and want the best for both our players and our dev teams. Our job isn't to be rock stars, but to showcase player contributions and highlight the amazing work that the developers (programmers, designers, artists, and others) do each day.

It can be difficult to explain the variety of things a good CM does. None of us went to school to be a CM. Many of us gravitated toward it because of our skills and love of working with gamers. We come from journalism back-grounds, social work, and customer service. Many have been teachers, event planners, or have worked retail and hospitality.

While we have a lot of "soft skills" (I hate that term; it implies they are less valid), we also have to understand tech. We use many of the same tools as developers; we learn CRM, JIRA, all kinds of project management software. Plus we must learn publishing tools, audio/visual software and hardware. We have to write well. We have to speak well. We have to keep on top of every social media tool to see if it works. Where are your players gravitating? Do you need a YouTube channel? An official Tumblr? Which outlets should you shutter as players stop using them?

Yet this is work that is consistently undervalued. It's not surprising to hear from players who don't understand that we aren't content creators, "All you do is tweet all day. Why aren't you fixing the game instead of posting on Facebook?" Others think all we do is moderate forums all day. Many have no idea that there are different levels of jobs in community, some more special-ized than others.

And even more surprising (and disappointing!), some people within the industry have just as simplistic an understanding. Often marketing/public relations/studio heads focus only on tangible results, not moods and sentiments. But when you try to attach a number to community, you're doing it wrong. Simply growing your follower count on social media, or tallying the number of "likes" you get, doesn't reflect whether you have a supportive, engaged community who will continue to buy and recommend your product. An engaged community will weather the ups and downs of game production (delays, a disappointing sequel, etc.), and will report their problems for the team to fix instead of abandoning the game. For games with multiplayer, social components, or an onxgoing DLC release schedule, a strong community is a must. Simply getting players to spend the money to buy your game isn't enough; the goal is to keep them playing long past the release date, sharing their love of the product with their friends, and waiting eagerly for your next release.

Ageism

I love what I do. I don't want to do anything else. I'm older than everyone I meet in this field, and I don't care. I certainly don't feel old. But getting older can be a real drawback in an industry as youth-obsessed as gaming. It's a constant worry: Did I get passed up on that last gig because I'm older? Do younger bosses think I'm less flexible or don't understand games and players?

I wouldn't be a community manager if I wasn't flexible, or didn't enjoy the stupidest memes, or get choked up at the sappiest in-game marriage between players. Because in creating a community, boundless enthusiasm is at the core of what I do.

How Can I Help?

As a community professional, I am always working to make other people's experiences better. Recently, I decided to help *us*. I had been cheerleading efforts to get community management taken seriously within the industry. I have always been outspoken—and somewhat demanding—to industry organizations that don't recognize community management. Thankfully, these efforts paid off and we now have a community management special interest group in the IGDA[2] and a Community Management Summit at GDC.

Through it all, my whole career, the key has been simple. I like to ask, "How Can I Help?"

It bothers me when people complain, "but why can't they do X, Y, or Z?" without rolling up their sleeves and getting it started. When I want something to change, I step up and ask how I can help. What can I do to get the effort off the ground?

I was encouraged to create the community management SIG when I spoke to IGDA staff. I was asked to be on the CM Summit Advisory board.

I accepted both challenges. This has been the most rewarding part of my experience in the game industry. Taking the lead and getting others involved. Highlighting the amazing people in my field, and putting the spotlight on them.

While I've been doxed and harassed, I still love games and I love my industry. But I want it to be better. Better to women, better to folks who are older, better to marginalized developers. From QA to Execs, we need to see more diverse voices.

Including an old broad like me. And maybe you.

Endnotes

1. Doctors Ray Muzyka and Greg Zeschuk, founders of BioWare.
2. The International Game Developers Association. This is the largest professional organization for computer and video game developers in the world. They have a robust system of "special interest groups," or SIGs, in which developers interested in particular topics like community management, writing, or women in games can meet like-minded individuals and exchange ideas through mailing lists and Facebook groups.

25

"Just a CM ..."
Why Community Management Is Judged So Harshly

Community management is the umbrella term for game company employees whose primary role is to interact with players directly. Their responsibilities range from policing company forums, to organizing fan appreciation days, to defending developers from fans thronging them at Comic Con.

Many game companies eschew a formal public relations (PR) department, preferring to cultivate a more personal relationship to their fans, giving community managers the sometimes conflicting responsibilities of promoting the game or company, while protecting the developers from angry or threatening fans.

Despite the fact that women are far more likely to be targets of severe abuse online,[1] 65% of community managers are female.[2] This can lead to ugly incidents, such as when *Mighty No. 9*'s community manager Dina Abou Karam introduced herself to the community with a piece of gender-flipped fan art, picturing the game's main character as female. A small number of outraged fans went on a spree against her "feminist agenda," posting her personal information in an accusatory video, and demanding a refund of their Kickstarter money.[3] Other times, fans may see community managers as "just a pretty face" put out by companies to appease them.

While other game developers who interact with fans do so by choice (and can stop at any time), community managers must have a visible, public presence, often under their own name and appearance. The Internet being what it is, this means that female community managers may have their looks continually judged, mocked, and discussed. Conventionally pretty CMs can find themselves assumed to be eye candy, while less conventional-looking women can find themselves under a constant barrage of fat-shaming, racism and general harassment.

To add fuel to the fire, even within game companies, community managers rarely receive the respect they deserve. Many developers, especially ones who have been in the industry a long time, see community management as part of marketing, and thus the enemy, or at best as half a step above fan forum moderators. Community Management jobs are frequently seen as entry-level, earning a median salary of only $48,462 across all tech fields according to Payscale.com's calculations[4], compared to $93,251 for a programmer or $73,864 for a designer in Gamasutra's annual salary survey[5]. (Community management is not tracked as a category in the game developer's survey, which kind of makes this point all by itself.)

Yet community management is the thin blue line protecting game developers from the cesspit of violence just outside their gates. It is the job of community management to read through the forums, determining which death threats against developers are actually just a bug report in disguise, and which are the product of a hateful or unstable mind and should be banned.

When a game community loses access to its community managers temporarily, as the children's game Neopets did over one June weekend, within 24 hours, their forums were dominated by threads like "about to start masturbating," "I would fuck all the adult swords on touken ranbu," and "how big is yr dick?"[6]

On the other hand, when a company invests in its community, as Riot has for *League of Legends*, a different picture can emerge. By carefully tracking negative behavior from its 67 million players, Riot learned that a full 87% of negative comments did not come from dedicated trolls, but "neutral and positive citizens just having a bad day here and there." By creating a system of Tribunals, in which players can report and judge each other for infractions such as racist slurs, Riot was able to reduce verbal abuse by more than 40%, bringing such incidents down to 2% of all games.[7]

But without such support, community managers can face a daily barrage of abuse with serious mental health consequences. CMs who break under the pressure often do so publicly, which makes a bad situation even worse.[8] Fortunately, the industry in general is starting to support community managers more, with GDC opening a Community Management track in 2014.

Becoming a Community Manager

Community managers often rise from the ranks of fans, and little formal training is generally required. Things hiring managers look for in a CM include:

- *Good Public Speaker:* Being a confident and engaging speaker at cons and trade shows is an important part of the job.
- *Good Written Communication Skills:* Community managers are a large part of game companies' PR. Blog posts and communications with fans must sound enthusiastic, but professional.
- *Media Contacts or Experience:* Community managers who have a background in journalism or other media can promote their game beyond the immediate community.
- *Game Knowledge:* CMs who are well-prepared with a background in the other games their community loves have a definite advantage when dealing with fans.

For Allies

If you're in the industry, try to support the community managers, male or female, who spend their days defending your work to the public. Some concrete ways to show your support include

- *Be Vocal:* Talk about the importance of community management in meetings with company leadership. Let the company know you value and appreciate their hiring experienced professionals to police your game/forums. When on forums and social media, speak respectfully to and about your community managers and make sure fans know they are respected professionals.
- *Ask for Feedback:* Get your CM's take on what did and didn't work in your game. S/he will have a fan's eye view of which complaints are the most frequent and justified.
- *Don't Stir Up Trouble:* When you interact with fans in your community, try not to throw something controversial on the fire, then go back to work. Consider asking the following questions before putting an opinion in writing: (1) Will it help the company's reputation? (2) Will it change anyone's mind? If both answers are no, consider whether it needs to be said.
- *Never Make Promises:* This one's for marketing. If you make a promise like, "This game has 36 endings," fans will remember. If you're wrong, or that number changes during development, community managers end up on the firing line for your mistakes.

Endnotes

1. Duggan, Maeve. "5 Facts about Online Harassment," Pew Research Center. 30 Oct 2015. Available at http://www.pewresearch.org/fact-tank/2014/10/30/5-facts-about-online-harassment/

2. Keath, Jason. "The 2012 Community Manager Report." *Social Fresh*, 2012. Available at http://www.slideshare.net/socialfresh/the-community-manager-report-2012. Note that this refers to general community managers, not game-specific, as there is more movement between game companies and tech companies than in some other fields.

3. Cheong, Ian Miles. "Be Respectful and Considerate—Mighty No. 9 Kickstarter Explodes with Misogynist Rage." *Gameranx*. 12 Dec 2013. Available at http://www.gameranx.com/features/id/19333/article/be-respectful-and-considerate---mighty-no-9-kickstarter-explodes-with-misogynist-rage/

4. Online Community Manager Salary (United States). 2015. Available at http://www.payscale.com/research/US/Job=Online_Community_Manager/Salary

5. "Gamasutra's Annual Game Developer's Salary Survey." 2015. Pages 2–3. Available at http://www.gamesetwatch.com/2014/09/05/GAMA14_ACG_SalarySurvey_F.pdf

6. Ashcraft, Brian. *Neopets* Community Melts Down: "Eat My Ho Butt." *Kotaku*. 29 Jun 2015. Available at http://kotaku.com/neopets-community-melts-down-eat-my-ho-butt-1714610137?utm_campaign=Socialflow_Kotaku_Facebook&utm_source=Kotaku_Facebook&utm_medium=Socialflow

7. Lin, Jeffrey. Doing Something about the 'Impossible Problem' of Abuse in Online Games. *<re/code>*. 7 Jul 2015. Available at http://recode.net/2015/07/07/doing-something-about-the-impossible-problem-of-abuse-in-online-games/?refby=gaminginsiders&utm_source=Gaming+Insiders+Weekly&utm_campaign=c953ebf884-The_Weekly_June_24th_2015s&utm_medium=email&utm_term=0_27af250667-c953ebf884-115726037

8. Andrews, Scott. "WoW Archivist: How Forum Trolls Broke a CM," *Engadget*. 16 Nov 2012. Available at http://www.engadget.com/2012/11/16/wow-archivist-how-forum-trolls-broke-a-cm/

26

Sheri Rubin

I Created My Own Path in Game Development ... And That's OK

50 Cent Bulletproof: G Unit Edition for PSP, Big Buck Hunter (BBH), BBH 2006: Call of the Wild, BBH: Shooter's Challenge, BBH: Sportsman's Paradise, Cafe Mahjongg, Carnival King: Big Top Shooter, Charlie and the Chocolate Factory, Club Pony Pals, Corner Pocket, Daytime Dollars, Decades, Finders Keepers (FK), FK Christmas, Golden Tee (GT) Classic, GT for PSX, GT Fore!, GT 2K, GT Fore! 2002, GT Fore! 2003, GT Fore! 2004, GT Fore! 2004 Extra, GT Fore! 2005, GT LIVE, Goldie the Gold Miner, Grandma Giddywinks, Mr. Biscuits—The Case of the Ocean Pearl, Realms of Gold, Sam & Max—Episode 1: Culture Shock, Episode 2: Situation: Comedy, Episode 3: The Mole, the Mob, and the Meatball, Episode 4: Abe Lincoln Must Die!, Episode 5: Reality 2.0, Episode 6: Bright Side of the

Moon, Shoe-B-Doo, Silver Strike Bowling, Tap Treasure: A Finders Keepers Adventure, Telepath Tactics, The Detail—Episode 1: Where the Dead Lie, Episode 2: From the Ashes, Touch-IT, Tower Conqueror, Word Spiral, and many more

Games Have Always Been a Part of My Life

Right now, imagine what you'd do if it absolutely didn't matter what people thought of you. Got it? Good. Never go back.

Martha Beck

Only a few months old and I was playing peek-a-boo—which, in reality, is not so much a game but a cruel joke on a baby's lack of object permanence. Next up was probably hide-and-seek; duck, duck, goose; and musical chairs.

Then there was *Q*Bert*, Go Fish, *Pitfall*, and freeze tag, along with *Super Mario Brothers, Aggravation*, Football (Soccer), and *Pac-Man*. It was a family affair as we played *Uno* and *Spades,* while holiday gatherings saw men versus women in *Trivial Pursuit.*

This love of games continued as I played computer, console, and handheld games, board games, *Dungeons & Dragons*, and MUDs.[1] But playing games wasn't the only place my travels would take me. I started "making" games early in life, too. I started small, through "modding," creating variations of classic games—see below for some of my advanced rules for *Candyland*! From there, I made analog games from scratch as a hobby.

Sheri Working on Some Early Designs

Candyland **Advanced Version #1:** *Candyland* gets boring if you're drawing and playing one card at a time, especially if you're stuck on a square for a long time. Instead, take a cue from the "advanced" version of *Sorry!* and let players have three cards in their hand at all times to choose from. It adds a lot more strategy and a lot less frustration to the game.

Candyland **Advanced Version #2:** To add even more strategy to *Candyland*, especially for older children and adults, allow players to choose to play their card on themselves *or* one of their opponents. It adds the choice to play offensively or defensively and when combined with the rule change in version 1 adds a new dimension to the game!

It was competing in tournaments for a customizable card game, however, that put me on the path to professional game development.

And that's OK. Because it made me realize I could …

Turn a Passion Into a Paycheck

People grow through experience if they meet life honestly and courageously. This is how character is built.

Eleanor Roosevelt

It all started when my enthusiasm for the games and player community caught the eye of the card game company's top employees. For not one, but *five* of their games I was brought on as a product ambassador, tournament administrator, and playtester.

I helped demo games to stores and game groups; assembled, managed, and ran convention booths; conducted tournaments; and assisted with testing alpha versions of expansion sets.

Unfortunately, I wasn't paid much—and competing at world championship levels was expensive!—so I continued to keep a "day job," usually helping companies with accounting, customer support, and operations. I squeezed in my work on the customizable card games around my full-time job, classes, and other commitments.

Things changed a few years later, however, when I got my first video game job. This time it was my insatiable curiosity and attention to detail that piqued the interest of one of the co-creators of *Golden Tee*.

I would hang out after work at Incredible Technologies' office and putt around the virtual golf courses. It wasn't long before I asked for a paper and pen to log "bugs" I would find. Something inside me *had* to make sure the team knew about the glitches and typos I came across, even if I was only playing "for fun."

The team began to ask me for my feedback and I started to help programmers debug issues and even create my own detailed test plans. It was during one of my "way-too-thorough-for-the-average-person-to-want-to-do-for-fun" tests that the co-designer and company vice president asked what I was doing.

We discussed what I was attempting, and why, which apparently planted an idea in his head. A few months later he asked me, "Why don't you come work for us and start getting paid for what you're already doing for free?"

The answer was yes, of course, and thus began my first quality assurance (QA) job as I shifted to video game development. But those early habits and enthusiasm for contributing valuable work for free, just to help others, played a huge role in my life and career in the years to come.

And that's OK. Because I was already used to …

Doing More for Less

> *There is a stubbornness about me that never can bear to be frightened at the will of others. My courage always rises at every attempt to intimidate me.*
> **Jane Austen, *Pride and Prejudice***

Plenty of studies show women in any industry are likely to be paid, promoted, and listened to less than their male counterparts. By starting out making less (exactly how much less depending on the job), it means salary-based raises or bonus structures only put them farther and farther behind.

What women get *more* of is discrimination, condescension, harassment, and microaggressions. We constantly face systems and cultures that consciously or unconsciously get in the way of our and our employer's success.

The game industry is no different, unfortunately, and my experience has put many of those issues in my path over the last two decades. I have encountered circumstances where I was

- Paid dramatically less than my peers. This was never equalized, even when my superiors admitted the truth.
- Blocked from opportunities to grow, by a boss who feared female subordinates would "show him up."
- Kissed and touched inappropriately by coworkers known and reported for sexual harassment. None were ever disciplined.
- Interrupted, patronized, dismissed, and devalued; because "a woman couldn't possibly understand the full situation."

And the times companies assumed I knew the full situation? That was when they expected me to speak on behalf of my entire gender. Despite the fact that women are individuals with varied tastes and styles—just like men!—I was supposed to explain how *all* women play games, or what games *all* women would play. (Because it was unthinkable that women might play *all* types of games …)

Being compensated, respected, and recognized less than your colleagues is rough for many women, regardless of the field. In a predominately male industry like games, it can also be quite isolating, because when you're the only woman in the room you don't have anyone else who understands your experiences.

(Un)fortunately I am stubborn, and when combined with my intolerance for unjust systems, and a strong desire to make things better, that meant two things:

1. I would continue to do more for less in the name of advocacy, through mentoring and volunteering for employers, groups, and colleagues.
2. My attempts to shine a light on problems and work toward solutions would make those trying to ignore the problems uncomfortable or hostile.

These efforts probably have held me back in my career, even as they have pushed the industry forward. But as the quote often attributed to Winston Churchill goes: "You have enemies? Good. That means you've stood up for something, sometime in your life."

And that's OK. Because by being committed to my companies, communities, and causes I was …

Standing Up for Something

Have the courage to seek the truth and speak the truth, to stand up for the underdog, and to stand up against intolerance—even if yours is the lone voice doing so. Have the courage to trust your gut and your own moral compass—your innate understanding of right and wrong.

Katie Couric

Among game developers, I am probably better known for my efforts to make this industry better than for the many games I've helped develop. I've met a lot of resistance to the work I'm doing. Some organizations attempted to dismiss my opinions and block every effort to make progress in an industry so desperately needing progress. Other times, I experienced harassment and abuse, including phone calls, personal attacks, doxing, and the like.

Don't get me wrong, though. While the industry can be harsh it can also be immensely rewarding. There has usually been enough good to outweigh the bad:

> For all the people who said "girls don't play games," there were the excited faces of women and girls as they beat another level.
>
> For all the devs who said women can't make great games, there were friends standing at podiums accepting their "Best Game" awards.
>
> For each company I saw lay off women and minorities but no straight, white men, there were the female, LGBTQ+, people of color, and other colleagues I helped find jobs.
>
> For each time leaders I worked with completely failed their colleagues, there were hundreds of fellow developers battling right alongside me for a better way.

There are moments throughout the years that confirmed for me that I can, and will, make a difference:

> The students I mentored who became lead artists, lead designers, senior engineers, and even studio founders.
>
> The colleague who said if his daughter wants to become a video game developer the industry will be a more welcoming place because of the work I've done. (I'll admit this made me tear up.)
>
> The day I heard our team's five years of hard work paid off by securing the first-ever dedicated track for video games QA at an industry conference.
>
> The smile on a young Girl Scout's face when she said she now feels comfortable considering a STEM^2 career.
>
> The board chair who said on record that if it weren't for all my hard work he didn't think the organization would have survived.

I count myself lucky to have an amazing group of friends and colleagues who have supported me as I stood up for what I believed in, what needed to be done, and what had to be said.

My time as a game dev hasn't followed any kind of standard track developers are supposed to take. I often feel I've spent more time advocating for video games and game developers than I have actually developing games.

Even outside my advocacy work, I was never one to fit inside the box. I found what I liked most was helping others—people, teams, organizations, etc. Drawing upon my varied skills and experiences, I became a "Jill-of-all-trades," taking on new roles and challenges, creating my own path through the industry.

And that's OK. Because it was about ...

Making My Own Way

Why in the world should you march to any lockstep? The lockstep is easier, but here is why you cannot march to it. Because nothing great or even good ever came of it.
Anna Quindlen

I've been in nearly as many roles while developing games as the number of games I've worked on. Community manager, QA, customer experience, level designer, litigation support, writer, producer, branding consultant, operations, corporate communications director ... the list goes on.

I think I eschewed the traditional model of junior, mid, senior, lead, etc., for this multiheaded hybrid of roles because of who I am and who I've worked

Advocacy Groups for Women in Games

There are numerous nonprofit companies and groups that advocate for women in games, teach girls to code, or assist with protection against online harassment. A few notable ones are

The Online Abuse Prevention Initiative: Randi Harper, Zoe Quinn, Alex Lifschitz, and Sheri Rubin founded this company to reduce online abuse by studying abuse patterns, creating anti-harassment tools, and collaborating with tech companies to support their communities.

Crash Override Network: Zoe Quinn and Alex Lifschitz used their experiences as the bullseye for Gamergate to create this support group for victims of online abuse. They provide information security, public relations, threat monitoring, counseling, and advice for dealing with legal cases and law enforcement.

The Pixelles: This Montreal-based nonprofit holds events to teach women how to make and change games.

Dames Making Games: This Toronto-based nonprofit offers free events and resources for trans and cis women, queer and genderqueer game-makers.

The Code Liberation Foundation: This foundation offers free classes to women who want to learn to program and make their own games.

Girls Who Code: They provide support, camps, and classes to encourage high-school-aged girls to enter STEM careers.

Editor

with. When I've worked with larger companies, I was given a "standard" role, but was still the one asked to jump in and help when gaps were identified.

For smaller companies and clients, it was simply a matter of necessity. Small studios often can't hire a dedicated person for HR, project management, PR, user experience, or event planning. In places like these, everyone wears multiple hats or success just isn't possible.

> Don't let anyone tell you what job you *need* to take or what company you *have* to work for to "further" your career. *You* decide what is right for you and your goals.

Sure, there are advantages to designing your own route through life: it provides variety, challenges, and a chance to find out more about yourself. The disadvantages, though, come when you never seem to "fit the mold," and available opportunities shrink or others start to doubt your expertise.

And that's OK. Because, while walking this long and winding road, I knew somehow …

Everything Was Going to Be Better

> *There are women who make things better … simply by showing up. There are women who make things happen. There are women who make their way. There are women who make a difference. … There are women who change the world every day … women like you.*
>
> **Ashley Rice**

When you grow up enjoying activities and jobs where you're surrounded by men, it's possible to get used to being the only woman in the room. Oh sure, there will be bumps in the road—like the time my male opponent stormed out of a tournament when I won our match after he'd just told his friends I was "only a woman" and couldn't be *that* good. Beating him in a complete shutout with over half our time remaining probably didn't help!

But, sometimes your fellow travelers make things better, like

Being recognized by all my coworkers and given a coveted annual employee award.

A male colleague telling a teammate to shut up and listen to me because I did, in fact, know what I was talking about.

The friends, colleagues, and even strangers who reach out to say they appreciate my work, they no longer feel alone, they now have the courage to speak up, they enjoy developing games again.

To create inclusive and supportive environments for marginalized voices, leaders should

- Publicly praise their accomplishments
- Create a sponsor program
- Validate their opinions and ideas
- Make sure they are heard

Those experiences make the pain and the struggle worth it. Those times make me think things are starting to change. Those moments make me remember why I make games.

And yes, I do take on non-game clients, I do advocacy work on non-game issues, and I do sometimes wonder just what the heck did I get myself into!

Yet I also enjoy helping clients hit their launch date, I enjoy making my own games, and I enjoy the days when I look across the room and see I'm no longer alone.

And that's … much more than OK!

Endnotes

1. Multi-user dungeon, an early text-based precursor to massively multiplayer games like *World of Warcraft*.
2. Science, technology, engineering, and mathematics.

27

The "Average Player"
How Game Testing Departments Can Bias Their Results

"Quality assurance" is the non-game-industry-specific term for all software testers. Video game testers can run the gamut from three-month contract workers brought in to intensively test a game at the end of its production cycle, to full-time employees who "embed" with development teams to test systems and features from concept to launch. While some full-time quality assurance (QA) staff make testing their profession, often the role is seen as a stepping stone, the "quick and easy" route into the game industry.

This can certainly be true. Short-term testers are often in demand, and taking such a position can be an excellent foot in the door of a game company. However, by paying poorly and using "a passion for video games" as the major qualifier, staffing companies often ensure they hire the same kinds of testers over and over—usually young, male, self-described "hard-core gamers."

But the problem with filling your testing ranks with a lot of similar people who like similar things, is that it starts to feel like those are things *everyone* likes. This tends to lead to companies overvaluing certain aspects of gameplay (such as "challenging fights" or "freedom to explore") and undervaluing others (such as "easy to understand" or "able to complete in short play sessions"). Most often, it is new or casual players who get penalized, since they are least likely to be represented among game testers.

Additionally, when you're testing the same game for 40+ hours per week, a level may seem easy to you while still being too difficult for many players to complete. Or you may find that what you think is "obvious" in your game's user interface is not at all obvious to those brand new to the genre.

While this isn't strictly a gender issue, reports consistently show women make up approximately 50% of all game players and game purchasers; the average age of female players is 43 years old; and there are twice as many adult female gamers as young male games.[1] If your testers fail to include those demographics, you lose the chance to gain valuable insight into your player base.

A largely straight, white male group of testers is also likely to miss things that might be offensive or that could be changed to make a game more diverse, inclusive, or accessible. Adding different voices and perspectives to a QA team can challenge developers to think critically about questions like "Why are there no female selectable characters?" or "How will someone with red-green color blindness know they're about to cut the red wire and not the green wire on the bomb they have to defuse?"

Becoming a QA Tester

While getting paid to sit around and play video games all day is a great job pitch, anyone who thinks that's what the job *actually* entails is in for a rude awakening. However, if you don't mind spending days at a time trying to walk up a single broken staircase, here are the areas you should excel at to be in QA:

- *Great Interpersonal Skills:* Whether reporting a bad user experience or telling a lead programmer the release candidate is crashing, testers are often "the bearers of bad news." The best QA leads have a knack for developing relationships, so their feedback is received with gratitude, not dread.
- *Excellent Written Communication Skills:* Ever seen those reviews in the App Store that say "my character got stuck in a wall and now I can't do anything. Fix it."? No QA tester would file a bug report like that. If your character got stuck in a wall, you need to specify: What character? What wall? What do you mean by stuck? And what did you do right before it happened?
- *Attention to Detail:* Great testers notice the little things, catching typos, upside-down textures, or that little graphical glitch before the game crashes. Remembering the exact steps needed to reproduce an issue can save a programmer hours of work when fixing it.
- *Creative Destruction:* Good testers go out of their way to break games by playing them out of order, using weird equipment, or otherwise playing differently than the designers expect.
- *Adaptability:* The industry changes constantly as players embrace new platforms. Testers who can shift gears quickly may find their jobs more permanent than those who resist change.

Using QA as a Stepping Stone

While some companies let QA staff move to other disciplines, and others even expect them to move on, don't assume testing is your golden ticket to becoming a designer, artist, etc. For some people, QA gives them needed industry experience to jump to another discipline. But others find they're pigeon-holed into a position they hate, and have to work 10 times harder to prove they really *are* an artist or audio designer. Do your research before you take a job as a tester and find yourself "stuck."

For Allies

One of the best things you can do, regardless of who your testers are, is give your QA staff the respect they deserve. They work long hours at low pay[2] to make sure your work is playable and fun by the time it reaches the public. They are a critical part of game development and treating them like part of the team—versus locking them up in a separate building!—goes a long way to making the most of the developer/QA relationship.

Until it's been put through the QA wringer, no level, boss fight, conversation, or cutscene should be considered ready to ship. Although it's currently rare for QA managers to have veto power over releases, including their sign-off in your process can help keep embarrassing bugs, exploits, blowback, and bad press away from your door.

Some helpful steps you can take to improve the diversity and effectiveness of your testers

- *Specifically Ask for Diverse Testers:* If you go through a staffing company to hire testers or arrange focus tests, they tend to use stereotypes to guide their decisions. Unless you specify, "I want a mix of hard core and casual gamers," or "I want this focus group to include people who have never played an FPS," you will get the same old crowd you always have. Make sure those who hire testers, set up user research tests, and implement playtest sessions know both your current player base and what new players you are trying to reach.
- *Include Concerns about Diversity in Your Testing Plans:* Many studios find that by bringing QA to the table even during preproduction, they can provide feedback that helps developers avoid last-minute changes that set a game's schedule back for months. Make sure your QA team knows you want and value their feedback on nontechnical issues like, "I felt uncomfortable with the scene where the hero's girlfriend is

abducted." Allow test plans and gameplay feedback reports to point out offensive stereotypes or places that diversity could be easily added.

- *Recruit Testers in Diverse Locations:* Don't just advertise for testers on your standard gaming websites or among your company's family and friends. Search out diverse game communities, especially women, LGBTQ+, and minority groups, to increase your chance of a broader candidate pool.
- *Look for Warning Signs in Your Job Descriptions:* QA positions often use language in job descriptions that implies the company doesn't want anyone but young, straight, white men—e.g., "rock star," "frat house," "hardcore gamers only," the use of all-male pronouns or a focus on the long hours.

Then, once those new diverse candidates are hired, make sure they are working in an environment that doesn't drive them right back out again! Listen to people's opinions, don't assume they will blithely crunch for weeks on end to make up for schedule slips, and keep an eye out for inappropriate behavior (especially in how testers talk and treat each other—many "hardcore gamers" may have gotten used to the "trash talk" they expect online).

If your company hasn't created a respectful environment, then even if you find new hires to add diversity to your team, they probably won't stay for long.

Endnotes

1. 2014 Essential Facts about the Computer and Video Game Industry. *Entertainment Software Association.* 2014. Available at http://www.theesa. com/wp-content/uploads/2014/10/ESA_EF_2014.pdf
2. For an in-depth look at the difficulties game testers face, read Jimmy Thang's IGN article, "*The Tough Life of a Games Tester.*" 29 Mar 2012. Available at http://www.ign.com/articles/2012/03/29/the-tough-life-of-a-games-tester

28

Leigh Alexander

Columnist: *Edge* Magazine, *Kotaku*

Editor: *Gamasutra, Kotaku*

Founder: Offworld.com

I'm a person who writes about play and its creators. I write about the culture of games and game-making—I especially want to change the conversation about who games can be by and for, and what they can be about. It's okay to call me a "game journalist," but I've come to believe that the word "journalism" in conjunction with what people like me do is a misnomer.

The Beginning of Game Journalism

The early days of writing about video games brought us a collective of enthusiastic young dudes making eager treks among press junkets to look at trailers, or to play previews, or attend other lavish activities. The game companies and their PR departments intended to win over these inexperienced, easily excited young men with fancy things, so they'd be awarded a good score in the magazines. This was the culture in which my profession was conceived: Buy 20 pale 19-year-old nerds some lap dances so they feel like adults, so they feel like men, and they will write nice things about the new, fancy, expensive graphics card.

I think we started calling ourselves "journalists" as a signal that we wanted to do more than be dutiful couriers to that traditional hype cycle: A person who works at a game company says something, our pen hovers over a notepad, we glance at the PR, who nods yes, and then we write it down. Saying "I'm a journalist," and "I'm doing reporting," indicated some minor intention toward adulthood, some commitment to actually question the party line from time to time.

In the mid-2000s, "exposing" things, and getting in trouble with PR, was the thing to do. It meant you were really blazing your own trail. No matter how many previews of unfinished works you dutifully handed forward, and how many arbitrary number scores you put on games (nearly everything was an 8/10, 9/10 if you think your product-loyal audience might flip out otherwise), as long as you were fighting with PR people, you must be doing something brave and bold and new.

Becoming "I"

When I started writing about games nearly nine years ago, even using the word "I" in an article—your feelings, your experiences, your opinions—was considered somewhat radical. You were supposed to be a professional journalist, after all, which meant The Facts came first, even if The Facts were arbitrary qualities like whether something was good or not or whether the reader might like it. At first, I gained an audience for writing about sex games, particularly the strange and somewhat dark Japanese sex simulations people were sharing on underground message boards. I treated them not as embarrassing curiosities but as interesting ones, and because I was a woman I could get away with it without seeming too creepy.

I had a blog called Sexy Videogameland—it was 2006 and blogs were supposed to have weird, long titles—and I said I wanted my writing to make games "sexy," in the marketing sense. I was profoundly aware that video games were not cool, that they were a little sticky, that their rigid vocabulary was primarily designed for the stimulation of teenage boys, and that this rigid vocabulary didn't allow for the kind of conversations that I, a young adult woman, wanted to have about them.

Making myself available in this way—a woman who used "I" in all her posts, who talked about sex, who wanted more vocabulary in the way we talked about games—gained me an audience fairly quickly, but in a sense it was hard work of an old-fashioned kind that gained me a career. I took the jobs no one else was interested in, like reporting on virtual worlds companies and their various investors, writing announcements about new technology tools or shader updates or procedurally generated foliage for game developers to read. I covered conferences about games for education and social good. They were not sexy topics, but it was journalism work of a kind, even though I was not ringing Nintendo's phone 10 times a day digging for The Facts of their backwards compatibility plans or what have you.

I began writing lightning-rod opinion columns, and interviewing famous game developers about their creative approaches. I began going on podcasts and I very much believed I was knowledgeable and opinionated. The amount of attention my work garnered increased and became more complicated the more visible I was, but I mostly gained in confidence and in pride.

I gave talks. I challenged the status quo. I thought we needed to talk about game developers as human beings expressing themselves, not as lists of names responsible for shipping the product. I thought we needed to reject the idea of games as product at all, and develop a way of talking about them as a medium of play.

I thought that most things that were popular in games were embarrassing, and culturally irrelevant. I said a lot of these things out loud. I was considered very "controversial." The label "controversial" bewildered me, as I worked alongside a lot of weird, nerdy men with bold personalities. This was the era of The Angry Video Game Nerd, and of the snide and withering *Zero Punctuation* video game reviews, and dozens of other popular articles by defiant men who wanted to be like that. Alongside them, I was actually a little bit boring, I thought, a little bit straight-laced.

I knew very few other women. When people asked me about this, I said it didn't matter.

It Mattered

These days I probably have the distinction of being the longest-serving woman in game "journalism," and I am certainly the most well-known woman. It is a sort of hollow victory. I am still the most "controversial." I feel sad for the girl who worked so hard, sat in the front row of a sparsely attended engine technology talk, typing away til her fingernails chipped. She didn't know what was going to happen.

They were never going to let me out from under "woman." Every value that mattered to me, that I pushed so hard for, was always going to be subsumed by "woman" to them. The words they used to describe me—I was loud, I was abrasive, I was mean, I was upjumped, I was arrogant, I talked too much—all of these words would never be applied to my male colleagues for the same behaviors, for wanting the same things (when they wanted anything at all besides better framerates and for everyone to stop complaining about violence or gender issues or anything that got in the way of their monolith of fun). I was a critic in a field where criticism was not welcome; I was a woman in a field where women were not welcome.

It took me a long time to become a feminist. But once I began to pick at this thread of unfairness—the words I was called that others were not called, the way swatting away pasty drunk losers in lanyards in late-night event parties was part of my job and not others', the way any other woman who entered the room was suddenly a threat, expected to compete with you and to be compared to you—suddenly the whole fabric came apart. It was like watching a power grid come on, suddenly bleeding veins of light into the entire dark city.

The entire value system of my field, from the way we worked to the things we made—the dark rooms full of gyrating bodies, the pugilistic physics, the blood spatter, the junkets of helmet-faces and trotting armors and darkly chuckling lanyard-wearers—all of it was predicated on the idea that women were not welcome.

All of the "journalism," all the old newsman bravado my colleagues had levied at my space up until then had failed to uncover that fact.

I'm happy to say, a lot has changed over the last few years. I know lots of other women who write about games now. I am part of a movement of people who share the same ideas: What if games can be for everyone? What if they can be human and inclusive? What if they can be about sex, or sexuality, or personality, or trauma? What if they can be feminist, and still be loved, still be authentic? What if they have nothing to do with the id of the "gamer," a theoretical marketing category of regressive, entitled nerd men who love realistic weapons and flinging snot at women like me on the Internet?

What if, all along, it's been the old way—men marching among junkets doing journalism about framerates—that was inauthentic?

Brazen Opinions

I've become increasingly willing to provoke these questions, to put these what-ifs forward. I've become increasingly certain of them. At the same time, I am now less tolerant—candidly, I am not tolerant at all—of arguments otherwise. I recently received an e-mail from a stranger who was disappointed I don't open comments on my articles. The e-mail read: "There are valid rebuttals to your brazen opinions Miss Alexander." Ah ha.

In 2014, I wrote down a brazen opinion in an article: that "gamer" was an artificially enforced marketing category, a grotesque appeal to juvenile male power fantasies which had nothing to do with the act of play, or with the art of design. Moreover, I wrote, by catering to these sticky boy-heroes, by refusing to brook any conversation, any analysis, any criticism of games that would welcome adults, or women, or people of color—by prizing the "gamer," a gape-mouthed consumer who wears a headset, demands from creators "value for his dollar," and complains that numeric reviews are not "objective"—we were choking an entire precious medium to death.

I'd decided to publish this piece after watching my friend be abused in public by these self-identified "gamers." About a month before I wrote it, my friend Zoe, the designer of a modest but interesting text game about living with depression, called *Depression Quest*, sent me a Facebook message; she told me her creepy ex had written a massive, warped, and rambling confessional blog post about her, and she wanted to know if I thought the press would treat it as news.[1] I told her that she definitely shouldn't worry, and that nobody would care about her creepy ex or his blog post.

I Was Wrong

Probably the greatest indignity of my long career is that from now on, because I am a woman who writes about video games, people will always ask me about Gamergate. Because of Zoe's ex's blog post, "gamers" decided they wanted to assault women under the guise of an inquiry into "ethics," as if these attackers were literate enough to understand what ethics mean, what journalism is.

To be honest, what I wanted was for the game industry to take responsibility for the crawling horde of squalling, infantilized, controller-clutching sexist brats it had created by coddling young white boys and telling them that their capital-f Fun was the *very most important thing* of all time, and that no one should *ever* ruin it even a little with their inconvenient human rights and needs.

I wanted game developers to abandon the "gamer," both as a target audience and an identity, and make games for everyone else. For human beings and new audiences and people who think it's absurd to assault women over their milky, tepid understanding of "journalism" and what writers do in media.

I didn't think it was going to be that controversial an opinion. Actually, the main thing I worried about was being accused of stealing ideas; I'd read other "death of geek culture" pieces from male colleagues in games and other media over the previous days. What was happening to Zoe was so egregious that people were looking for explanations, and they found them inside the culture of the products we created and championed.

I read many pieces making the same case as me, which was that when *Game of Thrones* can become the most-viewed television series maybe ever, the "geek" is no longer a rare and protected class. That there is nothing *Harry Potter*-special about a person who assembles their interests out of the franchise-related products they obsessively buy. That being the kind of person who had lots of game consoles growing up actually makes you fortunate, not oppressed.

I did not invent any of these suggestions. I wasn't the first to say them. But it was my employer who was brigaded until one of our advertisers withdrew their campaign. (That advertiser, widely chastened in the mainstream media for bowing to a hate mob, managed to introduce a multimillion-dollar program to "fight sexism in tech," but has yet to apologize to me personally.) It was me who was abused and threatened, at times as much as the women I'd been trying to defend.

A Changing Landscape

I'm still suffering for speaking, just like Zoe is still suffering for what her ex did, and all the other women I know, many of whom are in this book, are still being remembered mostly for what men said about them and did to them instead of for what we said and did. That the word "ethics" ever entered into the situation is insulting and absurd.

Things are improving. Importantly, they are improving. On one hand, I would not be telling the truth if I said that I nurtured, unstained and undamaged, a blazing love of all things gaming after all of that. But I will say that for every e-mail I got about Miss Alexander's Brazen Opinions, I got five from supporters, from people who love playing games as much as I do (playing games; not "gaming," not "being a gamer," not lining up to buy products). The creative climate is richer than ever. I cannot kill the "gamer." But I have started something entirely new.

Today I run a website called Offworld. Most of the games we cover are free, made with simple tools, often by women and marginalized people. Nearly all of the columnists we publish are women, too. We connect the curious and the casual with the tools and resources to create their own works. We cover a world of games that is new, and inviting, and beautifully weird: There are games about growing plants, about haunted pyramids and giant hornets, underground bars where you mix drinks for ghosts, challenging works about the European refugee crisis, and so much more.

I think that is about the best I can do, as a "game journalist." I am not "doing reporting," I am not getting to The Facts. I just want the best way to channel my anger. I want the best way to fight back.

Endnote

1. Editor's Note: This was, of course, the beginning of what has become known as Gamergate, a backlash against feminism in gaming that has defined much of the past two years for women in the field. For a more in-depth look at Gamergate, see Chapter 30.

29

Mattie Brice

Writer: *Alternate Ending, Nightmare Mode, The Border House*

Independent Game Developer: *Mainichi, DESTROY ALL MEN, Blink, EAT, Mission*

Like many of my peers, I grew up in a time when it was possible to always live in a house with a video game console and computer in it. I don't have memories of a time before *Super Mario Bros.*, so video games were never really new or exciting, just a part of life. What I didn't realize then were the unique circumstances that let me say that.

Growing Up

My parents immigrated to New York City from Jamaica in the 1980s, my grandmother taking my father away in the dead of the night to escape political strife, then my mother, his high school sweetheart, following after. Grandma is comically matriarchal, so when my father applied to universities—the first person in my bloodline to get the chance— she pressured him to give up his dream of being a pilot in favor of the more financially lucrative computer science (CS). They drove all the way to South Florida, where I was soon born, sharing my birth year with my childhood favorite game series, *Final Fantasy*. Being a CS major, my father evolved into the prototypical nerd and shared the interests of the people in his program, setting me up to play console and computer games for years to come. My mother never really got along with technology, so I wonder where I'd be now if my father had pursued his piloting dream, never to enchant me with those pixels on a screen.

Growing up, all my friends played video games. Despite the contemporary narrative that games were traditionally played by white boys, I played with a diverse range of kids; boys played with girls, eventually spilling over to mostly girl groups who liked to go to arcades. We usually coordinated who would ask their parents for what console or games, and visit each other's houses to play the things we didn't have.

My best friend and younger sister liked first-person shooters, but I, still very anxious and jumpy, stuck to narrative heavy role-playing games from Japan, especially once I received a Sony PlayStation. I was about 10 years old, fascinated with the worlds and characters and storylines. Content ratings weren't enforced, so I was exposed to what might be called "mature" content now, but which inspired me then. JRPGs suited me fine, because they were extremely long and I could save up for the next game I wanted by the time I played the first a couple of times. PlayStation games from 1997 to 1999 are my "golden era," that particular point that every person who grew up with games pines to return to. Many of my contemporaries look to an earlier time, fueling the current indie aesthetic that pays homage to the difficult platformers of the NES or western computer role-playing games (RPGs).

My early love for writing came out of fanfiction that I wrote about my favorite games, typically making two boys fall in love and ending in some rather clumsy smut. I wrote constantly; some I would trade with my friends, but a lot I kept private as I explored my relationship to gender and sexuality, which I wouldn't have words for until Wikipedia. There came a time though, sometime in high school, when the role of video games in my life started to fade. I had a PlayStation 2, but ended up spending my allowance going to the mall. My best friend and I would play *Dance Dance Revolution* and share appetizers at the Cheesecake Factory. Console and computer games started taking a back seat in my life.

Online Reality

Around that time, I became engrossed with reality TV shows like *Survivor* and *Big Brother*, fascinated by the social engineering which the game structure of the competitions brought out. I found communities who replicated the structure of these shows online, using free forums and AOL Instant Messenger. Online reality games, sibling to the more visible and more co-opted alternate reality games, facilitated my growing up, forcing me to think hard about ethics, to balance the selfish with the moral, and to navigate through online intimacies and betrayals.

I didn't know it then, but that was when I became a game designer, hosting both ORGs and chat room games of my own creation. A lot of my current design sensibility stems from my experience playing these intense social manipulation games. Coupled with my on-again, off-again relationships with massively multiplayer online (MMO) games, I always had a distinct focus on the social aspects of play.

Games again dipped out of my life when I started university, working 40-hour weeks, and struggling with my gender identity. I remember selling PlayStation 3s at Target and thinking that I could never afford a video game habit. Near the end of my undergrad years, I had to take critical theory courses in English and Sociology because of differing degree requirements between the creative writing program I dropped out of and the one I picked back up when I began living more purposefully as a queer woman.

I remember feeling spiteful, wanting to concentrate on fiction writing and become a mystery novelist. But when I got to these classes, my teachers allowed me to write papers on any form of media, even video games. The prospect interested me; no one else in my classes thought to apply critical theory to games. So, with a new proficiency in feminist analysis, I went back to my favorite games and unpacked much of the messaging I received when I was young. In one memorable class, my teacher actually showed games in class for us to write about. The two games, Emily Short's *Galatea* and Tale of Tales' *The Path*, convinced me that games were worth turning back to, and are still an inspiration today.

This culminated in a fateful research paper I wrote on gender identity and sexuality in games, using *Bayonetta* and *Persona 4* as examples of contemporary tensions surrounding the representation of marginalized identities. Academic writing on games at the time concentrated on huge landmarks, typically *World of Warcraft* or *Second Life*, so I started looking online for other criticism of games. To my surprise, I found a thriving blogging scene around game criticism!

I knew there were game reviews and previews, but had never encountered more thoughtful, in-depth writing on games before. After I graduated and applied to grad school, I wanted to start a food blog so I could get into lifestyle and entertainment writing as a side thing while continuing school. Discouraged by the apparent requirements of a camera and constant flow of pretty recipe posts, I decided to focus on games to practice writing regularly until I could afford a camera. I wanted to fill a need for more critical analysis of games from a social justice perspective, just for a few months, before getting deep into grad school. But those months turned to years and led me here.

The Blogosphere

I started with my own blog, *Alternate Ending*, and pitched to the feminist community blog *The Border House*. My work read like an undergrad literature paper, citing theorists, making claims, proposing new nomenclature. I leaned heavy on traditional feminist analysis that looked at where and how women and marginalized people appeared in games and the patterns of depiction and behavior around those figures. There was little other work on the topics I touched, which made me notable and helped me engage more prominent writers on social media. Within a short few months, my writing was all over the place: *PopMatters, Nightmare Mode, Ctrl+Alt+Delete, Kotaku, Paste Magazine*, and highlighted on *Gamasutra* and game criticism's hub, *Critical Distance*. Like many of my peers, a lot of my writing focused on the narrative of games, but since I also wrote and designed creatively, I tapped into the craft of games in a way few critics were doing.

It's hard to talk about the start of my, I guess, "career in games," since it often doesn't feel like one. Gaming in general is a volatile space; no one expects it to be fully formed or look the same year-to-year. Everything is new or surprising, still in an awkward teen phase. My path fits into that, a strange outcropping of circumstance that I – and others – have no idea what to do with. It's both scary and exciting: you can create something out of nothing, but there's little support for those not in the club.

Like much of the work done by and about marginalized people, my game criticism was done for free for a solid two years. I subsisted off a Starbucks paycheck and then the little financial aid I got in grad school. There is a very particular gauntlet people go through in order to get paid well to write about games: You start off doing grunt news work, writing up press releases and other boring reportage. Once in a while, you'll get to review a game that no one else wants or an interview at a major event. Eventually, you get to do more interesting news, better games, and feature work, and if you're lucky and schmoozed your way into someone's heart, you get hired full time and eventually get op-ed freedoms.

Game journalism didn't really have room for me, a nobody doing work reserved for op-eds, especially on then-derided social justice topics. Back in 2011, it was still "debatable" if the game industry was really sexist, so paying me to write about feminism in games, much less about being multiracial, queer, trans, and other marginalized identities, was out of the question. So I hustled, writing more than I do now to get noticed by someone, anyone.

I built a presence for myself on Twitter, which in itself was maturing, unaware of the dark habits it encouraged. I'm actually amazed at the visibility I managed to get in such a short time. I didn't even mean to go into social justice topics themselves, just use them as a lens for critical theory. But to my surprise, the head of my undergrad's lesbian, gay, bisexual, transgender, queer, and Intersex (LGBTQI) center followed my work and invited me to keynote their lavender graduation ceremony, to talk about continuing activism after school. I'd never thought of myself as an activist, and activism on social media was a new thing. This was when I realized I might have an actual role to play, inciting change instead of producing commentary.

Activist

A few months after I started my blog, the game criticism sphere started a fundraiser for me to attend GDC, the central North American event where game devs and writers mingle, sort of an industry Christmas. I had never been to a convention before! I managed to get a press pass that said "Blogger" and had only one assignment: to preview a game called *Girl Fight*, a bland fighting game about barely dressed women. But it was a turning point for me. I met a lot of peers and people I looked up to, industry figures who would later pull for me. I was unnecessarily shy around veteran journalist Leigh Alexander (Chapter 28), who acquainted me with games fairy godfather Richard Lemarchand, both of whom would later become friends. I left GDC with multiple contacts who asked me to speak at future events, including IndieCade, PAX, and GDC itself.

Games started to take over my life. I traveled to Boston, Los Angeles, Seattle, and Austin within the span of months, a pleasant shock as I had never been able to afford to fly more than once every two years. What could I make of all this? I still didn't anticipate a career in games, so it was unclear what it all amounted to. But I really enjoyed speaking and would accept many, mostly unpaid, speaking gigs as I tried to work this out.

Around this time, the rumbles of the now-titled DIY/queer games movement started to draw notice. I met anna anthropy at GDC and through her met a network of people who shared similar radical values. We traded development tips and made a wave of iconic games about queer experiences. During a week between conferences, I worked on my first digital game, *Mainichi*, a game I describe as a note to my best friend about the struggles I had with my gender and the depression that caused.

When I put *Mainichi* on the Internet and linked it to my social network, I expected a few followers to play it and then move on. But, to my surprise, it resonated with people, enough to be held up as one of the games symbolizing this new movement. Soon I started writing more about design and theory, and became more than a critic and activist. I don't even know how to describe what I do outside of a long list of activities I have a hand in. So now I just settle for "artist." I continued to get speaking engagements and eventually my work was exhibited in galleries and at conventions.

I stepped up my involvement with community service. I co-founded the Queerness and Games Conference at University of California, Berkeley, a free event that uses school funding to subsidize costs. I also co-organized Lost Levels, a radical unconference held during GDC that was open and free to all. I still find events to help out at, mainly other people's conferences and game jams. Providing accessible avenues to connect with games reminds me why there is a need for activism in games—not just to keep the industry responsible, but for the people on the ground floor who rarely get opportunities to express themselves.

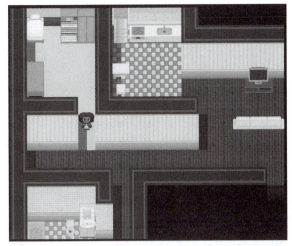

House Scene from Mainichi, *©Mattie Brice, 2012*

You would think that having more speaking credits than most editorial teams would give me an edge in game journalism. But that was still a dead end. Editors found the topics I wanted to write too risky, or said I was too new to give paid op-ed spots. The field was shrinking, with many sites closing down and few opening, a big game of musical chairs where established names got the new positions and there were fewer and fewer spots to break in. After a couple of failed attempts to get regular paid work, I tried to crowdfund my own eccentrically named publication, *re/Action*, which taught me that there isn't a lot of attention paid to the growth of game criticism (and that getting a group of writers together to work on a project is an absolute nightmare).[1]

As I started to come up dry, Patreon launched, the first long-term crowd-funding platform for artists. Being one of the first people from games on there, I started to make money straight from my readers and fans. Soon I was paid more than any publication could offer me (which still wasn't much, especially compared to rent costs in the Bay Area). But it was something; I could get paid regularly just to write. It wasn't what I expected, but with this, I could form a base for something else.

Leaving Games

I continued, and continue, to feel distant from the game industry. Once I made my own money, I started to see how unsatisfied I was writing things I didn't care about. Games have a lot of potential, but companies often waste it doing the same old thing. I became interested in artsier games, especially nondigital ones. I got involved with pervasive/theater game scenes and began to look for connections to play in other fields I enjoy, like fashion, food, and architecture. Most of my lasting connections were in games academia, centered mostly in New York City, leaving me continually isolated.

Then, Gamergate.

I gained a large following of harassers who stalked and threatened me at every turn. I was walking on eggshells, always unsure what would set off the mob. Because of how activist celebrity works on Twitter, what happened—and still happens—to me went largely unreported.

Street Scene from Mainichi, *©Mattie Brice, 2012*

I'm sad to say that my story ends with me disavowing the game industry for its lack of support and non-stance on the continuing harassment. When I opted to write about more unusual kinds of play and avoid the digital, people eventually stopped reading and following me as closely, and I felt alone in coping with what was happening.

I couldn't find work; companies and institutions didn't find my experience credible or valuable, and I don't come from any sort of wealth to help me fund a new venture or education. I've spent the last year feeling defeated, crushed that all the work I just described amounted to nothing.

I don't think my story, at least its general themes and trajectory, is particularly unique; rather, I am one of the few who gets to tell it.

Marginalized people face glass ceilings and revolving doors at extremely high rates in this industry. Now that it's socially acceptable to speak about social justice, publications and companies are jumping on the bandwagon to benefit from shallow motions to support the struggle many people live. But I was there before all these people put rainbows on their logos. And it's people like me who pay the price for progress, in whatever little form it may come.

Endnote

1. Editor's Note: Except these writers! This book has been a delight to work on.

30

Anita Sarkeesian and Laura Hudson

The Phenomenon of Gamergate

Anita Sarkeesian: Creator of the nonprofit Feminist Frequency and the *Tropes vs. Women in Videogame* webseries

Laura Hudson: Writer at *Slate* and *Wired*, editor at Offworld.com

People often ask why Gamergate happened in video games and not another form of mainstream media—whether this terrifying campaign of online harassment against women emerged from the fandom of games in particular, or whether it was some sort of fluke.

The abuse meted out by Gamergate is a diverse catalog of horrors: sending rape threats, death threats, and bomb threats to their targets, Photoshopping them into pornography, publishing their home addresses, e-mailing their employers en masse demanding their termination, harassing their families

and friends, and even sending heavily-armed SWAT teams to their homes.[1]
The goal of the harassers is simple: to systematically intimidate and abuse
their targets, creating a hostile environment intended to drive women out
of the industry, or silence them altogether.

So What *Is* Gamergate?

The harassment of women in video games is nothing new. Although the
horrors perpetrated by Gamergate elevated the issue to national visibility,
female developers and critics within the gaming industry have been regularly
targeted for harassment by misogynist cyber mobs for years.

The Gamergate movement, which finally allowed many of these harassers to unify and coordinate under a loose banner, can be traced back to
an August 2014 blog post by a man named Eron Gjoni. The lengthy dia-
tribe accused his ex-girlfriend, independent game developer Zoe Quinn, of
having sex with multiple men in the game industry in exchange for positive reviews about her free game *Depression Quest*. Though the accusations
were quickly proven baseless and false, the inflammatory nature of the post,
which combined lurid accusations about Quinn's sex life with the specter of
"corruption," immediately made Quinn a target for the swaths of angry gamers who already resented the presence of women in gaming culture.

Although there was no truth to the accusations against Quinn, many
within the Gamergate movement latched on to the idea of "corruption
in journalism" as a more palatable cause than unvarnished misogyny, and
tried to reframe the goals of the movement as being about "ethics in video
game journalism." Perhaps unsurprisingly, these concerns rarely delved
into any actual ethical issues—including the sometimes questionable
practices of multi-million-dollar game development companies manipulating the gaming press—but instead remained obsessed with digging into the
personal lives of women in games, threatening and harassing them.

The burgeoning wave of abuse soon enveloped numerous other female
developers, critics, and fans, especially targeting trans women and women
of color. It drove some from their homes, after their personal addresses
were posted online alongside death and rape threats, and drove others from
the industry entirely. Gamergate's attacks became so vicious and destruc-
tive that mainstream media started to take notice, attracting coverage from
The New York Times, *The Colbert Report*, *Newsweek*, *Time*, *USA Today*,
and *Last Week Tonight with John Oliver*. The national media attention initially

afforded to Gamergate has waxed and waned as new high-profile instances of harassment emerge[2], but the daily unreported harassment of women in games continues.

The Monster We Created

But Gamergate was not an accident. In many ways, Gamergate is the monster that the mainstream game industry created, the darkest and most pernicious expression of the values it has tacitly endorsed for decades and the entitlement it has marketed to and cultivated in a primarily male audience. It's also in part the collateral damage from the decisions about who is catered to, who is treated as fully human—and who isn't.

What lies at the heart of Gamergate is not a nebulous concern for "ethics," as some have claimed, but rather a profound sense of insecurity and emasculation at the idea that the world of games might no longer be an exclusively male fantasy domain, or that the sexism that informed straight men's exclusive hold on the imagination of this culture might no longer be tolerated.

It's worth asking, perhaps, where they came by this disproportionate sense of entitlement in the first place. While part of the answer is surely rooted in society at large, part lies within the culture of games themselves.

The overwhelming majority of mainstream games are made by, for, and about men; they are fantasies that center on male characters and male desires, where men are the heroes and female characters are typically relegated to secondary positions as sidekicks, sex objects, and helpless damsels in need of rescuing.

In one NIH study,[3] 42% of the box art for video games displayed exclusively male characters, while only 7% featured only female characters. When women did appear, they were scantily clad or sexualized 61% of the time. Other marketing and advertising for games is similarly designed to cater to heterosexual men, evoking fantasy worlds where men are heroes and women are secondary and sexualized, if they exist at all.

The sense of entitlement this elicits is so pervasive as to often be invisible. For a gamer to look across a sales rack at a video game shop and see primarily white, male characters toting guns on the covers—and women who are scantily clad, if they are present at all—is not only unremarkable, but entirely expected.

Indeed, the problem is not merely that these games exist, but that their dominance has become so ingrained that any deviation from this focus on straight, white, heteronormative men is viewed as a form of injustice.

A Changing Industry

Over the past decade we've seen an exciting increase in the number of women and girls playing games, as well as more widely accessible gaming formats like mobile and casual games.

But in the eyes of many who consider themselves "hardcore" gamers, titles that aren't oriented toward competition and violence or aimed at their particular demographic are dismissed as "not real" games, and the people who play them—especially women—are labeled as "not real" gamers. Any attempt by the industry to acknowledge women's interest in games is viewed as invalid and opportunistic, motivated by "political correctness" and an affront to games culture worthy of vituperation. But their most aggressive responses and sustained abuse are reserved for women who challenge the status quo of games as a male-dominated space.

The hostile and sometimes violent reaction to the idea of female players being recognized or catered to within games is a demonstration of what sociologist Michael Kimmel calls "aggrieved entitlement": the frustration and rage experienced by the dominant members of a group when the special advantages and benefits they enjoy feel threatened. For some male players, this exclusive, unquestioned focus on the stories, desires, and power fantasies of men is not only normal but obligatory; anything less is robbing them of something they believe they are owed.

"When that sense of entitlement is aggrieved," writes Kimmel in his book *Angry White Men: American Masculinity at the End of an Era*, "they don't just get mad; they get even."

The idea of women muscling in on what "should" be men's exclusive territory or attempting to "take their games away" by criticizing the status quo and demanding space of their own is perceived by these men as profoundly unjust and emasculating. And challenging that sense of entitlement can be a dangerous thing indeed, especially in a culture where men are taught to respond with aggression and even violence when their masculinity is threatened. And that's exactly what a small but vicious contingent of gamers have tirelessly devoted their energies to doing, by harassing women relentlessly and brutally until—they hope—the women fall silent or disappear from their view.

Of course, the pervasive issues of sexism, objectification, and male entitlement are not unique to games. Indeed, many of the problems that plague gaming culture are merely culturally specific reflections of the systemic gender issues that plague our society at large. But they are filtered and amplified by the culture that surrounds games, where men are catered to and women are marginalized, men are depicted as heroes and women as sex objects, and men are taught to expect that everything should be for and about them, while women should consider themselves lucky for whatever they can get.

Inaction Means Support

While some in the game industry, especially independent studios and developers, took vocal stands against Gamergate, the responses from many of the most prominent companies and individuals came too late or not at all. Their reasons varied: some said they didn't want to draw more attention to the harassment; some bought into the idea that the harassment campaign was about "ethics"; some feared that Gamergate might turn on them as well.

But there's another more insidious reason that more developers, publishers, and journalists didn't speak up: because the business of games is in many ways built on the same foundation as the entitlement that fueled that harassment. Indeed, the video game industry sells billions of dollars worth of entitlement to young men each year, and thus they have billions of reasons not to challenge it, even when it manifests in horrifying ways.

Although some claimed that their refusal to speak out against Gamergate wasn't the same as complicity or endorsement, their silence sent a message regardless, not only to the harassers it emboldened, but to all the women in games who watched their colleagues' abuse pass without censure from so many of the men they respected within the industry.

It was this climate of entitlement and "neutrality" that helped embolden the nascent Gamergate movement, particularly in the critical early days when it first started to gain momentum. By the time the abuse became so obvious and extreme that it started receiving mainstream media attention, it was already too late; there was no way to put the genie back in the bottle. Far from being neutral, the silence of so many in the game industry wasn't neutral at all: it was a powerful message, and in many ways the same message it had been sending all along.

A Culture of Fear

To this day, Gamergate's harassment campaign against women in games continues on a daily basis, a scourge that continues to drive women from an industry where they are already vastly underrepresented and to discourage others from participating for fear of becoming the next target.

This sustained climate of fear has rippling consequences, some of which will be invisible to us until years down the road. Gamergate's regressive movement helped equip many disaffected young men with terrifying skill sets and tactics for harassing and threatening women online, particularly by manipulating the weaknesses of online platforms and law enforcement when it comes to dealing with digital abuse. What long-term impact will they have, particularly on the targets who end up in their crosshairs in the future?

For many women in the industry, Gamergate has eroded their sense of personal and professional security; they now worry about their safety when attending gaming events and conventions, or fear becoming the next target when they speak up about the problems in the industry or simply speak about their work. Even beyond the women who have actively left the game industry, how many more aspiring creators and fans now feel reluctant to join it when they see how it has treated women?

Rather than a brief attack that lasted only as long as its mainstream visibility, Gamergate remains a constant presence and an ongoing threat to women in games culture. This makes it a continual call to action for the gaming industry: not only to do more to combat this specific hate campaign, but to challenge the larger environment of male entitlement and female marginalization that allowed it to flourish.

The late historian Howard Zinn famously said, "You can't be neutral on a moving train." It is time for the industry to take a long look in the mirror and decide what it wants to be and what it wants to represent: a space where the male-dominated status quo remains unchallenged and even aggressively defended, or a progressive space where people of all genders are welcomed and treated with respect.

Endnotes

1. SWATting is generally accomplished by calling in a false report telling police there were gunshots or suspected terrorist activity at the home address of an innocent victim.
2. Abad-Santos, Alex. "SXSW's Gamergate Debacle, Explained." *Vox Media.* 29 Oct 2015. Available at http://www.vox.com/2015/10/29/9635348/sxsw-gamergate-harassment
3. Near, Christopher. "Selling Gender: Associations of Box Art Representations of Female Characters with Sales for Teen- and Mature-Rated Games." U.S. National Library of Medicine, National Institutes of Health. 1 Feb 2013. Available at http://www.ncbi.nlm.nih.gov/pmc/articles/PMC3586322/

31

Conclusion

Editing this book has been like a literary box of chocolates. Each time I opened a new file, there was a different delicious story. Some were sweet. Some were tart. A few were unexpectedly spicy. But all were unique and fascinating.

If there is one thing you get from reading this book, I hope it is to recognize that there is no single narrative of being "women in games." All of the thousands of women who work in games are as unique and as driven as the ones whose stories you've just read. But though the characters change, the setting is the same, and the hostility and ignorance we have all faced continue to be a defining part of many women's experience of games. To change that setting will require effort on all fronts:

- Audiences for existing games need to protest racist and sexist material, not to drive those games off the market, but to help them improve their sequels.
- Audiences for alternative games must "vote with their dollars," buying games that speak to their interests and showing that such markets exist and can be profitable.
- Women in games must speak out together against unfair practices and poor working conditions and support each other when doing so puts any one of us in the line of fire for abuse.
- Men in games must actively seek out the opinions and skills of their female colleagues, take steps to hire more female candidates, and be aware that a "poor culture fit" on a co-worker or potential female hire might only be a hidden prejudice reminding them that "she's not just like me."

- Game company executives, like executives in all technology companies, must make workplaces that are more family friendly; that punish sexist behavior with an eye to eliminating it, not just avoiding legal liability; and that choose to market games as accessible to the broadest possible audience, rather than scrambling for a greater share of the single narrow slice of young white men.

Fortunately for us, that change is already underway. While the events of the past two years have been brutal and discouraging, they are bringing about much-needed change. GDC has added Advocacy as a main track, of equal stature with Programming or Art or Design, and panels such as the #1reasontobe are often packed with supporters. The 2015 IGDA Leadership Summit had 16 female speakers out of 40 (near parity!).

Gamergate blew the ugly secrets of game industry misogyny into the broad light of day for the first time, and we all learned that public sentiment was solidly with the victims of harassment. On *Law & Order: Special Victims Unit, The Colbert Report, Last Week Tonight with John Oliver,* and many other mainstream shows, female game developers were given the spotlight as either heroes or unlikely victims of circumstance, while those who were willing to threaten real women with rape and torture over video games, or willing to commit "the deadliest school shooting in history[1]" to avoid having to listen to Anita Sarkeesian (Chapter 30), were dismissed by the public as the grotesque SVU-villains-of-the-week they are.

So, help us. Take the suggestions in this book and do your part to change the industry we all love and depend on. Make a game, play a game, share a game, critique a game; these are the things we all do, for fun or as jobs. And if every one of us does them a little more mindfully, we can make an industry with room for diversity in both its audience and its creators.

This is the twenty-first century. Games are first coming into their own. Virtual reality is finally in real development, and in 2015, for the first time, people in America spent more time engaged in mobile apps than watching television.[2] As the current generation grows up with iPads attached to their fingers before they're out of diapers, it is inevitable that this is the century in which interactive media will overtake traditional.

So, let's stop using a twenty-first-century medium to fight nineteenth-century battles for equality. Games and interactive storytelling are about to become the new movies, and like movies, they will need to expand to find every kind of audience: comic book games, action games, and horror games, but also romantic comedies, period dramas, and quirky character pieces.

In the end, we will know games have reached their full potential when we retire the word "gamer" from our vocabulary. In a world where games exist for every type of player, the word "gamer" will have no more meaning than the word "movie-goer" or "TV-watcher," because everyone will play games. And the only question left to ask will be, "Which one is your favorite?"

Further Reading

While most of the specific research underlying this book was done online, there were other books which inspired me to do this project. If you want to read further about the issues women face in games and tech, or the ways that games and female players interact with each other, you might be interested in

> *Lean Out:* edited by Elissa Shevinsky. OR Books. A collection of essays about women's experiences in start-up, tech, and venture capital.
> *Maxed Out: American Moms on the Brink*, by Katrina Alcorn. Seal Press. A riveting combination of personal memoir and well-researched indictment of the anti-family policies of American business.
> *The State of Play: Creators and Critics on Video Game Culture*, edited by Daniel Goldberg. Seven Stories Press. A look at how the politics and culture of games intersects with reality.
> *Beyond Barbie and Mortal Kombat: New Perspectives on Gender and Gaming*, edited by Yasmin B. Kafai, Carrie Heeter, Jill Denner, and Jennifer Y. Sun. The MIT Press. An academic look at gender in gaming. A follow-up to 2000's *From Barbie to Mortal Kombat*.
> *Women and Gaming: The Sims and 21st Century Learning*, by James Paul Gee and Elisabeth R. Hayes. Palgrave MacMillan. An academic approach to how gaming can motivate real-world learning.
> *You're Never Weird on the Internet (Almost):* by Felicia Day. Touchstone. Felicia Day's funny, touching memoir ends with her own brush with Gamergate, which showed many gamers that even the well-loved and consistently sunny spokeswoman for geek culture could suddenly find herself in the crosshairs.

Endnotes

1. Ahmed, Saeed. "Anita Sarkeesian Forced to Cancel Utah State Speech After Shooting Threat." CNN. 15 Oct 2014. Available at http://www.cnn.com/2014/10/15/tech/utah-anita-sarkeesian-threat/
2. Perez, Sarah. "U.S. Consumers Now Spend More Time in Apps Than Watching TV." *Tech Crunch*. 10 Sep 2015. Available at http://techcrunch.com/2015/09/10/u-s-consumers-now-spend-more-time-in-apps-than-watching-tv/#.3sgmhp:WkD0

Index